"Bruxy Cavey and I agree that religion is a terrible category in which to place the Christian faith. In these masterfully reasoned pages, however, Cavey argues that Jesus himself was so opposed to the rules, regulations, rituals, and routines of organized religion in his day that his followers would do well to emulate his attitude and instead follow his wonderful 'subversive spirituality' of faith active in love rather than wooden obedience to the dictates of organized religion. Cavey is not advising us to flee the organized church; he's advising us to ward off any claims that it provides the exclusive way to God. This is excellent, cautionary reading for any thirsty readers who might mistake the cup (the church) for the life-giving water it contains (Jesus' true teachings)."

— DR. PAUL L. MAIER. professor of ancient history,
Western Michigan University; author of
In the Fullness of Time

"Bruxy Cavey is a dynamic and creative thinker. He understands the ways in which the radical and liberating message of Jesus addresses the matrix of postmodern society and the deepest needs of its citizens. *The End of Religion* captures Bruxy's deep sense of what is going in culture and how the life and teaching of Jesus relates to life on planet Earth."

— DR. JAMES BEVERLEY, author of *Religions A to Z:
A Guide to the 100 Most Influential Religious Movements*;
professor of Christian thought and ethics, Tyndale College &
Seminary; associate director Institute for the Study of
American Religion Santa Barbara

NavPress Deliberate

From the very beginning, God created humans to love Him and each other. He intended for His people to be a blessing to everyone on earth so that everyone would know Him (see Genesis 12:2). Jesus also taught this over and over and promised to give His people all they needed to make it happen—His resources, His power, and His presence (see Matthew 28:20; John 14:12-14). NavPress Deliberate takes Him at His word and stirs its readers to do the same—to be the children of God for whom creation is groaning to be revealed. We have only to glance through the Bible to discover what it looks like to be the blessing God has intended: caring for the poor, orphan, widow, prisoner, and foreigner (see Micah 6:8; Matthew 25:31-46; Isaiah 58); and redeeming the world—everyone and everything in it (see Colossians 1:19-20; Romans 8:19-23).

NavPress Deliberate encourages readers to embrace this holistic and vibrant Christian faith: It is both contemplative and active; it unites mystery-embracing faith with theological rootedness; it breaks down the sacred/secular divide, recognizing God's sovereignty and redemptive work in every facet of life; it dialogues with other faiths and worldviews and embraces God's truth found there; it creates culture and uses artistic ability to unflinchingly tell the truth about this life and God's redemption of it; it fosters a faith bold enough to incarnate the gospel in a shrinking and diverse world. NavPress Deliberate is for everyone on a pilgrimage to become like Jesus and to continue His work of living and discipling among all people.

Become what you believe.
The NavPress Deliberate Team

ENCOUNTERING THE SUBVERSIVE
SPIRITUALITY OF JESUS

THE END

OF

RELIGION

BRUXY CAVEY

NAVPRESS◑

NavPress is the publishing ministry of The Navigators, an international Christian organization and leader in personal spiritual development. NavPress is committed to helping people grow spiritually and enjoy lives of meaning and hope through personal and group resources that are biblically rooted, culturally relevant, and highly practical.

**For a free catalog go to www.NavPress.com
or call 1.800.366.7788 in the United States or 1.800.839.4769 in Canada.**

© 2007 by Bruxy Cavey

All rights reserved. No part of this publication may be reproduced in any form without written permission from NavPress, P.O. Box 35001, Colorado Springs, CO 80935. www.navpress.com

NAVPRESS and the NAVPRESS logo are registered trademarks of NavPress. Absence of ® in connection with marks of NavPress or other parties does not indicate an absence of registration of those marks.

ISBN-13: 978-1-60006-067-0
ISBN-10: 1-60006-067-6

Cover design by The DesignWorks Group, Charles Brock, www.thedesignworksgroup.com
Cover image by Getty
Creative Team: Melanie Knox, Don Simpson, Reagen Reed, Arvid Wallen, Pat Reinheimer, Kathy Guist

Unless otherwise identified, all Scripture quotations in this publication are taken from Today's New International® Version (TNIV)®. Copyright 2001, 2005 by International Bible Society®. All rights reserved worldwide. Other versions used include: the *Holy Bible,* New Living Translation (NLT), copyright © 1996, 2004. Used by permission of Tyndale House Publishers, Inc., Wheaton, Illinois 60189. All rights reserved; the *New Revised Standard Version* (NRSV), copyright © 1989, by the Division of Christian Education of the National Council of the Churches of Christ in the USA, used by permission, all rights reserved; the *New American Standard Bible* (NASB), © The Lockman Foundation 1960, 1962, 1963, 1968, 1971, 1972, 1973, 1975, 1977, 1995; the *Good News Bible Today's English Version* (TEV), copyright © American Bible Society 1966, 1971, 1976; the *Contemporary English Version* (CEV) © 1995 by American Bible Society. Used by permission; *The Holy Bible, New Century Version* (NCV) copyright © 1987, 1988, 1991 by Word Publishing, Dallas, Texas 75039. Used by permission; *THE MESSAGE* (MSG). Copyright © 1993, 1994, 1995, 1996, 2000, 2001, 2002. *THE MESSAGE* Numbered Edition copyright © 2005. Used by permission of NavPress Publishing Group; and the *King James Version* (KJV). The author's paraphrases and translations are marked as PAR.

Published in association with the literary agency of Alive Communications, Inc., 7680 Goddard Street, Suite 200, Colorado Springs, CO 80920 (www.alivecommunications.com).

Cavey, Bruxy, 1965-
  The end of religion : encountering the subversive spirituality of Jesus / Bruxy Cavey.
      p. cm.
  Includes bibliographical references.
  ISBN-13: 978-1-60006-067-0
  ISBN-10: 1-60006-067-6
  1. Apologetics. 2. Religion. I. Title.
BT1103.C38 2007
230--dc22

                            2007015650

Printed in the United States of America

3 4 5 6 7 8 / 11 10 09 08

TO MOM AND DAD,

WHO ONCE ENCOURAGED MY SEARCH,

THEN CELEBRATED THE RESULTS,

AND NOW THINK ANYTHING I WRITE

MUST BE WONDERFUL

Contents

PART THREE: The Irreligious Implications

A Rest from Religion

But I still haven't found what I'm looking for.

— U2

Our world is full of people on a quest for ultimate reality—truth seekers who are moving toward spirituality as quickly as they are moving away from religion.

For these seekers, religion seems too narrow or too rigid to hold all of the truth they are searching for. They are open to learning from all religions, but reluctant to commit to any. Often they reject religion for one simple reason: They have had firsthand experience with it. Many have been part of an organized religion in the past, and the experience seemed more burdensome and boring than freeing and enlivening. They resonate with Lenny Bruce, who said, "People are leaving the church and finding God."[1]

Perhaps some of this describes you. My wish is that this book has fallen into the hands of someone who is not just an inquiring skeptic but also a spiritual seeker. *I am writing to people who may have grown tired of religion but are not prepared to jettison the idea of connecting with God.*

If you can relate, I would like to suggest a focal point for your quest, a point of reference to help you sort through the multitude of spiritual alternatives available today. Consider the possibility that Jesus Christ is in an unparalleled position to offer spiritual help for all people, regardless of their religious background. Think of it. A rabbi to the Jews, a prophet to the Muslims, an avatar to the Hindus, an enlightened one to

Buddhists, the Son of God to Christians, a wise teacher to secularists, and "a friend of sinners" for the rest of us. Is this coincidence? Unlike any other religious leader, prophet, philosopher, or spiritual guru, Jesus alone is positioned to deliver a message to all people of all religions and no religion. This means that, regardless of your present worldview, Jesus could be the perfect place to start your search.

To be clear, I am not talking about the Christian religion versus all other religions. Take one look at church history and you will see that Christianity needs to hear the message of Jesus as much as or more than most religions. No, I am talking about the person of Jesus, transcendent of any one religion and a light for all. If you are investigating spiritual truth, I believe Jesus can offer you the guidance you are looking for.

I am fascinated by the fact that no matter how hostile people are toward organized religion, especially the Christian religion, these same people often tend to have a soft spot in their hearts for the historical Jesus. Sure, they may recast Jesus in their own images as someone who supports their own ideas of God, but that shows all the more their desire to adopt Jesus into their lives. They want Jesus to be on their side. Even though the Christian religion repels them, they know enough not to blame Jesus. It is as if something resonates with their hearts about this figure of history. Why are so many books written and read about Jesus? Why does "the Christ-figure" emerge as significant in worldwide myths, novels, plays, and poetry? Why are you reading this book? What is it about Jesus that is strangely attractive?

One of my favorite contemporary thinkers, John Stott, confirms this unusual appreciation for Jesus in today's world: "Indeed, there are many people who are critical of the church yet who, at the same time, retain a sneaking admiration for Jesus. In fact, I have never yet met anybody, nor do I expect to, who does not have a high regard for Jesus Christ."[2]

Brian McLaren fleshes out this idea a little more in his thoughtful book *The Secret Message of Jesus*:

Think about the people who—even though they've given up on "organized religion" due to bad or boring experiences with it—still have a high opinion of Jesus. Or maybe "opinion" isn't the right word: what they have is a certain sense of *possibility* regarding Jesus, a sense that there might be more going on with him than most people realize, including perhaps many who call themselves Christians.[3]

Could it be that God still has something to say to us through Jesus that we have not made room for yet? Is it possible that God will not let us marginalize Jesus, no matter how disturbing or irrelevant we find the Christian religion?

Religion can be tiring—a treadmill of legislated performance powered by guilt and fear. At the same time, generic spirituality can also be a tiring enterprise because it lacks a focal point. Many people who have rejected religion have turned to a kind of smorgasbord spirituality that allows them to pick and choose their belief system as they go along. Don't get me wrong, I love a good buffet (and I've got the body to prove it!), but what works for food does not necessarily work for faith. Many of these spiritual taste-testers are also weary of a search that has come to lack focus and foundation. They feel bloated but malnourished, fed up with empty spiritual calories.

It is to people like many of us—tired of religion and perhaps tired of our own striving to find alternatives to religion—that Jesus says the following words: "Come to me, all you that are weary and are carrying heavy burdens, and I will give you rest. Take my yoke upon you, and learn from me; for I am gentle and humble in heart, and you will find rest for your souls. For my yoke is easy, and my burden is light" (Matthew 11:28-30, NRSV).

Notice that Jesus is not pointing toward a different and better religion, but instead he invites us to *himself* as an alternative to the weary way of religion. This is a prominent theme in his teaching, and one that we will examine in more detail later. For now it is enough to ask:

If Jesus is somehow God with skin on, God himself coming in person *to us*, what might the radical implications be? Does this not completely reverse the direction of humanity's spiritual pursuits? Religion is exposed as our attempt to reach God, and the climb is tiring. But if Jesus is God coming to us and becoming one of us, then religion is redundant.

Religion uses *rules* to force our steps, *guilt* to keep us in line, and *rituals* to remind us of our failure to live up to those rules. In doing this, religion adds more weight to those who are already burdened with life's hardships. But Jesus offers us the *rest* we're searching for.

Because these words of Jesus capture his invitation to us all, I'd like to quote them again, this time from a different version called *The Message* by Eugene H. Peterson. Here is your chance to do more than read, to drink in words that speak to the heart of our deepest human longings. Read these words of Jesus slowly and thoughtfully to see if they resonate with you:

> "Are you tired? Worn out? Burned out on religion? Come to me. Get away with me and you'll recover your life. I'll show you how to take a real rest. Walk with me and work with me—watch how I do it. Learn the unforced rhythms of grace. I won't lay anything heavy or ill-fitting on you. Keep company with me and you'll learn to live freely and lightly." (Matthew 11:28-30, MSG)

I want the "rest" that Jesus offers here. I want to learn the "unforced rhythms of grace."

Although Jesus does offer rest, please notice that he says, "*take my yoke upon you*" (TNIV), not "take my couch underneath you." He offers rest, yes, but it is active, constructive, creative rest. Yokes are farming implements put on the necks of animals so they can pull a plow or wagon. A yoke, then, is a symbol of purposeful work and cooperative labor. I say "cooperative" because a yoke often unites two animals, working side-by-side, together in rhythmic teamwork. Perhaps Jesus wants us to picture him alongside us in the yoke, or perhaps he is pointing to the fact that we grow best spiritually when we move forward in a partnering relationship with others. Either way, Jesus promises that there will be work involved if we want to learn from him, but it will be the kind of creative, purposeful, and *partnering* labor that is more of a release than a responsibility, like life back in the days of the Garden of Eden (see Genesis 2:15).

I am excited to be a part of the growing movement of people who are discovering this rest that Jesus offers from the legalistic demands of religion. Because the spirituality of Jesus transcends any one religious institution or tradition, people around the world with various religious backgrounds or no religious background are coming together to learn from this unique figure of history, and now you are invited to join the dialogue.

Acknowledgments

Whether through a store or a friend, you have somehow come across this book. I'm grateful this has happened, even though I may not know whom exactly to thank. So for now, let me begin by thanking *you*. Assuming that you may actually press on to read at least some of what lies ahead, I'm grateful for your time and partnership in this endeavor. Whether or not we agree on all points, I hope that the time you spend working your way through this book might play a role in generating fresh thinking and healthier living regarding spirituality, faith, and the person of Jesus. In my opinion, these are the kinds of subjects we should be reading more about as a kind of investment in eternal things. And if you actually paid good money to purchase this book, then let me thank you for contributing to a worthwhile cause—the Cavey family mortgage fund.

I am also grateful to the many people, seekers and skeptics alike, who, after hearing me speak or reading an earlier edition of this book, offered thoughtful questions and honest feedback. You have helped me grow through this project. Thank you for your questions and your challenges, as well as your generous affirmations.

Sometimes when I talk about the origins of this book, I end up using "we" language. I talk about why *we* wrote this book and what *we* are hoping people will get out of it, etc. No, I'm not talking about God and me, although (at the risk of sounding wacko right off the bat!) I do have a sense of divine participation in this process. I am also not using the royal "we," as when the Queen says, "We are not amused." Rather, I'm speaking about friends at my church, The Meeting House. I am a member of a team of volunteers and staff who work side-by-side, each doing his or her part to help bring about good things in people's lives. The message of this book has been forged within this spiritual community. We could not fit all the names on the front cover, so even though this book is "officially" written by Bruxy Cavey, those of us who are a part of our church know better. To all of you who are on this journey with me at The Meeting House, thank you for helping me experience and express this message.

Right. Now it's time to mention some names.

I'm indebted to particular authors for igniting my passion for Jesus studies. Among them are N. T. Wright, John Stott, Dallas Willard, Philip Yancey, Robert Capon, Gregory Boyd, and others whose works appear in the bibliography. Most recently, I have been encouraged by Brian D. McLaren's book *The Secret Message of Jesus*. If you haven't read it yet, I recommend this book as a wonderful follow-up to reading *The End of Religion*. Beyond that I would also recommend N. T. Wright's book *Simply Christian* and John Stott's *Why I Am a Christian* as great next steps in your journey toward Jesus.

I am not a writer. I believe in the message of this book, and the message is what drives me, rather than a love of writing. This book exists only because of the input and encouragement from an amazing group of friends who have invested time in me and this message. Nina, Greg, Daniel, Chris, Michelle, Hans, Lucy, Ken, Suzie, Tricia, Karen, Melanie, Melissa, Natalie, Salina, Roger, Ruslana, Tim, Tom, and Peter. Thank you all!

Rick Maranta worked as my editor on a previous edition of this book and has continued to get in the trenches with me to help me achieve greater clarity and simplicity in my writing style. His fingerprints can be found all through this text. Thank you, Rick.

It didn't take long after meeting my "Deliberate" editor at NavPress, Don Simpson, for me to realize that he is a deep soul with a penetrating mind. Don, I am privileged to have you as my editor for this project and, more so, as my friend. I'm also grateful to be in a process of getting to know Caleb Seeling, senior editor of Deliberate. Thank you, Caleb, for the leadership and uncompromising vision you bring! Reagen Reed has served as my copy editor, and I appreciate her fine work along with the contributions of so many others at NavPress.

Tim Day and Rich Birch are copastors with me at The Meeting House and have invested countless hours in getting this message to print and into your hands. Thank you both for your partnership.

Beth Jusino is my agent south of the border (that means the United States to us Canadians). It's a joy to journey with you, Beth! (Now get back to work.)

Over the past few years, I have been blessed with a particular friendship of unsurpassed quality. Most of the chapters in this book were at some point a conversation between Greg and me before taking written form. Thank you, Greg, for showing me a passion and thoughtfulness for the irreligious message of Jesus that motivates me to write.

My daughters, Chelsea, Chanelle, and Maya, are my heroes. Thank you for being such terrific people! It is such a privilege being your dad!

My wife, Nina, takes what this book presents as concepts and puts skin on them. She lives the life and mentors me by her example. In her life I see, I mean really *see*, Jesus. I am so blessed to be able to live with this woman! I love you, Nina. In the words of one of our favorite bands, The Choir, "Baby I love your mind."

Finally, I want to thank Jesus himself. Rumor has it that Jesus of Nazareth didn't stay dead after his crucifixion. So, just in case Jesus happens to be reading this, let me end these acknowledgments by putting it into print—thank you, Jesus, for the faith, hope, and love you offer each of us.

The Holy Hand Grenade

1 . . . 2 . . . 5!

— MONTY PYTHON

There are basically two kinds of people in this world. Those who like Monty Python and those who can't figure out what all the fuss is about. I am in the first group and find *Monty Python and the Holy Grail* to be one of the funniest movies I know. (If you're a Monty Python fan, then I'm sure we've just experienced a deep inner connection. Thanks for bonding. If not, I'm sure you're giving me one of those "I just don't get you" looks that non–Monty Python fans give Monty Python fans — but please, bear with me!)

One of my favorite scenes in *Monty Python and the Holy Grail* is when King Arthur and company use the "Holy Hand Grenade" to blow up the nasty bunny with big teeth (not quite as scary as the demonic-looking bunny named Frank in *Donnie Darko*, another of my favorite movies, but now I digress).

Oddly enough, I think the phrase "Holy Hand Grenade" could apply to the Bible, a document designed to blow up religion from the inside out, with the teachings of Jesus functioning as the pin. So when you pick up a Bible, consider that you are holding an explosive device.

Of course, I'm not talking about a physical explosion or a book that sanctions religious terrorism. I'm talking about a book that contains a message with the power to dismantle religion's grip on our world. I realize this point of view might contradict everything you have thought about the Bible and that I have some serious explaining to do. So I'd better get to it.

The Bible is far more than the religious holy book for two major world religions — Judaism and Christianity. It is a library of ancient documents that point toward a surprisingly nonreligious spirituality that ultimately culminates in the subversive message and mission of Jesus. Although embraced by many religious institutions as their founding Scripture, the pages of the Bible reveal an *irreligious* agenda, one that is designed to explode religion from the inside out. I am convinced that the Bible holds clues to a way out of our slavish addiction to religious systems, while it simultaneously invites us into a direct connection with the Divine.

But isn't the Bible a book full of rules, regulations, rituals, and routines — the very stuff of religion? True, the many texts of the Bible, especially those of the Old Testament (that part written before Jesus), do contain laws and rituals, systems and institutions. But these religious ideas are not its starting point or its ending point. The Bible begins by painting a picture of the ideal world — a world *without* religion, a garden where God and people live in naked intimacy. This was God's original intention for humankind. In the Bible, it is only after people turn away from his ideal of mutual trust and intimacy that God gives them rules and routines, traditions and teachings — but this is not the end of the story. The rules and rituals of the Bible are like a map that leads to a great treasure, though they are not the treasure itself. I think this is what the revered Jewish poet and philosopher Abraham Joshua Heschel is driving at when he says, "Religion as an institution, the Temple as an ultimate end, or, in other words, religion for religion's sake, is idolatry."[1]

Religious people often tend to confuse the treasure map for the treasure.

The final chapters of the Bible describe where God is leading the world — back to the garden, to a world where religious rituals and institutions are noticeably absent.[2] Between the opening and ending chapters of the Bible, a subplot unfolds of how poorly people have responded to the rules and routines of religion. Yet ultimately, every page of the Bible points toward or reflects back on the coming of Jesus, the one who intends to put an end to religion and to point a way back to the ideal of the garden. And that is, in brief, why I see the Bible as a Holy Hand Grenade, for it invites us into a way of living that makes religion super-fluous, exploding its monopoly on access to God.

The Jesus described in the Bible is scandalous. He is not portrayed as the founder of a world religion, but the challenger of all religions. He is a subversive, anti-institutional revolutionary. Now, when I say "anti-institutional," I am not suggesting that Jesus opposes all forms of organization, but that he opposes dependence on any one organization for our connection with God. I did not form this conclusion based on piecemeal evidence from marginal sources. Nor did I have a mystical experience through which I was given divine truth. We can leave those approaches for other books by other authors. I am writing about the compelling picture we see of Jesus in the Bible itself.

As we will discuss in the following chapters, *the primary mission of Jesus was to tear down religion as the foundation for people's connection with God and to replace it with himself—the Divine coming to us in our own context and our own form. This is what Jesus called "the kingdom of God." It is God and his people, living together the way he originally intended.* For this reason, much of what Jesus did and taught only makes sense when we realize that his stated goal of offering salvation to the world (see Luke 19:10) also included the abolition of religion as a competing system. When we understand this, the New Testament writings come alive with invigorating energy. The stories Jesus told, the arguments he engaged in, even the healings he offered, all helped to demolish the smug assumptions of the religious people of his day and to destabilize their dependence on the system.[3]

As the subtitle of this book suggests (*Encountering the Subversive Spirituality of Jesus*), I want to focus on the role Jesus plays regarding religion and spirituality—calling us out of the one and toward the other. I hope this book will serve as a first step for those who want to investigate

Jesus and will help people who already consider themselves Christians to recalibrate their thinking about the biblical Jesus. A follow-up book called *The Irreligious Life* will paint a picture of what your life might look like if you were to fully embrace and live out this subversive spirituality as your own.

We have a variety of approaches available to help us get back to the original teachings of the historical Jesus who lived about two thousand years ago.[4] For the purposes of this book, I will be intentional about using the Bible as my primary source, for two important reasons. First, the four different Greco-Roman biographies of Jesus we have in the Bible (called the Gospels) are historically more valid than many of us have been led to believe. Scholars debate how closely we can date the Gospels to the events they record, but all measure the gap in decades, not centuries. To put this into perspective, our earliest writings about the Buddha date from approximately five centuries after he lived. [5]

But there is another reason I'm using the Bible as my primary source for this book. It is the fact that religious people, at least those from the Christian tradition, must take a *biblical* message seriously. The Bible is the authoritative Scripture for Jews and Christians, and a book respected by Muslims and others. Yes, the many extrabiblical, Gnostic gospels have captured the interest of the general public today, but my purpose in this book is to point out the radical nature of the message of Jesus that has been sitting right under our religious noses all this time. It is right there in the gospels of Matthew, Mark, Luke, and John. Rather than invite people to consider newer texts or sort through complicated and often-unsubstantiated theories about Jesus (of which there are many), I hope to show how the Bible itself points toward the irreligious nature of Jesus' message and mission. I want to explode the popular myth that the Bible presents a conservative Jesus who supports (and is a product of) the institution, while the Gnostic gospels and other ancient texts introduce us to a more radical Jesus who challenges the institution. [6]

Simply put, my goal is not to invent a new spirituality in the name of Jesus, but to help you unearth buried treasure—a perspective on

Jesus that comes directly from the Bible itself. Although it has been covered over by centuries of religious rubble, together I want us to clear a path back to the original intent of Jesus' words and works. We will certainly not be the first to do this, but sadly, we will be part of a minority in the history of the Christian faith.

You may believe the Bible is the inspired Word of God, or a historically valid collection of documents, or just one of many ancient texts from which we can receive some understanding of the historical Jesus. Regardless, the Bible can be the perfect starting point for investigating Jesus, especially because the religious institutions that most desperately need to hear his explosive message already embrace it. Religious leaders have for too long forgotten the Bible's dangerous implications and have enshrined it as an innocuous artifact on display at a local church building near you.

Yes, I think this Holy Hand Grenade has been lying somewhat dormant for two millennia, and it is high time we pulled the pin.[7] Therefore, my hope is to make my case from the Bible itself, rather than presenting a theory that tries to discredit the Bible to make its case.

With that in mind, as you make your way through this book, you will notice the text is peppered with references to the relevant Bible passages. If you are interested in digging deeper into these topics, look up the references, read the context, and continue your own investigation. The book you are holding can be a quick read or a launching pad into deeper investigation, depending on what you want out of it. To that end, each chapter concludes with a "Q & Eh?" section (hey, I'm Canadian) to help generate personal thought, dialogue with a friend, or group discussion. I especially encourage group discussion because of my conviction that personal spirituality grows best in the soil of authentic community.

The book is laid out in three sections. The second section (along with chapter 1) is really the heart of the book. These chapters make up an examination of the irreligious teachings and actions of Jesus. If delayed gratification is not your forte, then by all means, jump right to it. Part 1 sets the stage and lays out the issues at hand. Part 3 begins to wrestle with how all of this applies to our lives.

I should also take this opportunity to mention that I use the male pronouns "he" and "him" in reference to God with both regret and conviction. The Bible does not teach that God is male. God is a Spirit, within whom maleness and femaleness both find their origin and identity (see Genesis 1:26-27; John 4:24). And here we encounter the limitations of language. English, like the original languages of the Bible (Hebrew and Greek), does not provide us with a gender-inclusive, singular, personal pronoun. And I don't want to refer to God in impersonal terms. (*He* is not an *it*.) Therefore, I use male pronouns because of my conviction that God is personal, not because I think he is male. Further, I wish to align my syntax with the ancient languages.[8]

Philosopher and compassionate activist Jean Vanier says, "I have learned that the process of teaching and learning, of communication, goes in two directions at all times."[9] My years of speaking on the topic of this book and living out the implications in spiritual community have taught me the same lesson. Now that I write my thoughts down to be read by people I may never meet, I hope the dialogue does not stop. Please be encouraged to write me with feedback, criticism, questions, stories, and, yes, even encouragement. And, if I am dead by the time you read this—a morbid thought but an honest one—then know that I look forward to getting to know you on the other side.

Q & Eh?

1. I claim we can see that the Bible is clearly an *irreligious* document because of its beginning, its ending, and its main character. What do you think about my argument so far?

2. What is the value of basing the irreligious message of Jesus on what the Bible says, rather than basing the same message on personal revelations, conversations with God, or ancient non-biblical literature?

3. Many religious leaders of Jesus' day missed the point of his teaching because their preconceived notions and institutional biases interfered with their ability to see and hear spiritual truth. Likewise, history reveals that many leaders of the Christian religion have superimposed their own agendas over the teachings of Jesus rather than submitting their lives to his subversive message.

   • As we start this journey, what do you think are some of *your* unseen biases or hidden agendas when approaching the topic of Jesus or the Bible?
   • How might they potentially cloud your view of truth?

4. What are you looking forward to (a) the most and (b) the least in the process of working through this book?

I did not see a temple in the city,
because the Lord God Almighty and the Lamb are its temple.

— REVELATION 21:22, NIV

———◆•×•◆———

PART ONE

THE
BEGINNING
OF
THE END

———◆•×•◆———

"Blessed is the person who is not scandalized by me."
— JESUS (PAR)

CHAPTER ONE

Water, Wine, and Scandal

*Act just once in such a manner that your action expresses that you
fear God alone and man not at all—you will immediately in
some measure cause a scandal.*

— Søren Kierkegaard

Let's play a word-association game. I say "Jesus," and you say . . .

If you were to take out a piece of paper and write down every word
that comes to mind when I say "Jesus," my guess is that *irreligious* might
not make your top-ten list. There was a time when it wouldn't have
made mine. But all of that changed.

I entered a season in my life when I began to realize that the Jesus
described in the Bible was far more attractive, exciting, and scandalous than the meek and mild Jesus many churches proclaimed. I was
young and beginning to study the Bible for myself and, in the process,
came to believe that I held a volatile document in my hands—one that
had the potential to destroy all religion from the inside out. Dorothy
Sayers writes, "The people who hanged Christ never, to do them justice,
accused Him of being a bore; on the contrary, they thought Him too
dynamic to be safe. It has been left for later generations to muffle up
that shattering personality and surround Him with an atmosphere of
tedium."[1]

I recall reading the story of my favorite miracle: the one where Jesus
turned water into wine (I know, it's your favorite too). I was thinking
about how Jesus used his power, not only to heal, but also to encour-

age the celebration of life. However, as I read more closely, I noticed something that initially puzzled me and eventually forced me to begin rethinking religion, spirituality, and what Jesus was all about.

I felt like I had walked onto the set of *The Da Vinci Code*. Like the characters who stare at Leonardo's painting *The Last Supper* to find clues to an ancient mystery, I was staring into a written passage of the gospel of John to find the meaning of something I had never noticed before. What I eventually saw was just a brief phrase revealing a small detail of the story, but it became a keyhole through which to peer into a larger reality.

I know I'm saying a lot without saying what I want to say. That's because I don't want to spoil the fun for you. See if you notice the same thing in this story. Look beyond the wine to see the scandal. And here is a hint: remember that Jesus did things that won the favor of common people, while at the same time enraging the leaders of the religious establishment.

Three days later Mary, the mother of Jesus, was at a wedding feast in the village of Cana in Galilee. [2] Jesus and his disciples had also been invited and were there.

[3] When the wine was all gone, Mary said to Jesus, "They don't have any more wine."

[4] Jesus replied, "Mother, my time hasn't yet come! You must not tell me what to do."

[5] Mary then said to the servants, "Do whatever Jesus tells you to do."

[6] At the feast there were six stone water jars that were used by the people for washing themselves in the way that their religion said they must. Each jar held about twenty or thirty gallons. [7] Jesus told the servants to fill them to the top with water. Then after the jars had been filled, [8] he said, "Now take some water and give it to the man in charge of the feast."

The servants did as Jesus told them, [9] and the man in

charge drank some of the water that had now turned into wine. He did not know where the wine had come from, but the servants did. He called the bridegroom over [10] and said, "The best wine is always served first. Then after the guests have had plenty, the other wine is served. But you have kept the best until last!"

[11] This was Jesus' first miracle, and he did it in the village of Cana in Galilee. There Jesus showed his glory, and his disciples put their faith in him. (John 2:1-11, CEV)

How is that for a wedding gift—six huge jars full of the best wine going! John records that these stone water jars could each hold between twenty and thirty gallons. This makes for a grand total of between 120 and 180 gallons of wine, which would fill over two thousand four-ounce glasses. Now that's a lot of party fuel![2] It's a nice way to enter the miracle niche market, don't you think? But this is just the beginning.

The New Testament (that part of the Bible written after the coming of Jesus) was written in Greek. The word translated *miracle* in verse 11 is really the word *sign*—something that points toward the true nature of Jesus' message and mission. This miracle is not just about providing refreshment for thirsty guests. There is more going on here.

Think about the radical symbolism involved in this event. The idea of miraculously turning water into a completely different liquid was not new to the people at this feast. As Jews, they would be intimately familiar with the story of Moses, the Lawgiver, who was granted the power to turn water into blood (see Exodus 4:9), a symbol of God's judgment. Now Jesus comes with the power to turn water into wine, a symbol of God's blessing and joy (see Psalm 104:14-15). Something is changing. In the Hebrew Scriptures, written long before Jesus' time on earth, God had prophesied that one day he would raise up a prophet "like" Moses (Deuteronomy 18:18).[3] "Like"—meaning similar in some ways, yet obviously different. Moses and Jesus offered people freedom from whatever enslaved them, whether Egypt on the one hand or sin and selfishness on the other. Moses achieved that freedom for God's people through demonstrations of God's anger and judgment. Jesus offered it by demonstrating God's grace and mercy. This is not to say that the God of the Old Testament and the one revealed through Jesus are at odds or contradictory. God simply responded differently to humanity at two different times in our development and in two different contexts. Examine any parent's relationship with his or her children over the years and you will see how radically the parenting style changes as the children mature and circumstances develop.

Of course, it is not out of the ordinary to acknowledge that Jesus' message was one of blessing and joy. But, as I continued to contemplate this "sign," I realized that Jesus was not just *adding to* established religious tradition through his miracle. He was subverting it. Did you notice the scandal?

Take another look at verse 6. John tells us that Jesus did not have the wine served out of ordinary wine jars. He directed the servants to use the sacred containers set aside for a religious ritual. When I investigated further, I found that one of the traditions of some religious groups of that day (especially those of an influential group called the Pharisees) was regular ritual hand cleansing. They would dip their hands in sacred water as a way of symbolizing a desire to remain pure from the sin of the world (see Mark 7:1-4).

But why would Jesus use these sacred stone jars for the water-turned-wine? There were undoubtedly other containers available that could have held the joy-juice. If they had just run out of wine at this party, there obviously would have been plenty of "empties" around to hold the miracle liquid. Wine jars, wine jugs, wine bottles, wine kegs, wine skins—whatever they had been using—were sitting right there, empty, waiting to be filled. So why the stone jars? Why the sacred icons of religious tradition? Why intentionally do something so potentially offensive?

I was faced with an unexpected but undeniable fact: *Through his first miracle, Jesus intentionally desecrates a religious icon.* He purposely chooses these sacred jars to challenge the religious system by convert-ing them from icons of personal purification into symbols of relational celebration. Jesus takes us from holy water to wedding wine. From legalism to life. From religion to relationship.

Jesus seems to be saying that his message of love—a radically accepting love—is too great to be contained by the old ways of religious tradition.[4] His new wine demands new wineskins (see Matthew 9:17).

I knew I had to let go of my religious assumptions and let the Jesus of Scripture be who the Bible says he is, and not whom two thousand years of church history and tradition say he should be. So began my intentional search for a three-dimensional Jesus, beyond the stained glass windows of the religion that bears his name.[5] I wanted to learn more about—and more from—the Jesus who thinks our world needs more wine and less religion. I now know that this one miracle story is simply the tip of an irreligious iceberg contained within the Bible.

The writers of the Gospels—the four biblical books that record the life of Christ—use a fascinating Greek word to describe the effect that Jesus routinely has on his religious audience. They describe Jesus as a *skandalon*, meaning a stumbling block, an offense, a scandal. Their point seems to be that Jesus is a rock, but one you can trip over just as easily as build your life upon. Anyone who holds too tightly to his or her religious preconceptions will sooner or later become offended at Jesus. Unless, of course, they do what countless Christians have done and tame the historical Jesus through years of conservative tradition.

Thankfully, the biblical record won't let the irreligious agenda of Jesus be so easily dismissed. His subversive spirituality was a way of living that he was willing to die for, and, as we'll discuss later, it was through his death that Jesus finally brought about the end of religion.

In part two we will explore more examples of Jesus' behavior and teaching that are *scandalous* to religious conservatives of every genera-tion. But before that, there are a few things that must be said, including the important business of clarifying our terms, as we'll do in the next chapter.

Q & Eh?

1. Let's get back to playing that word-association game.

   • I say "Jesus," you say . . .
   • Why do these particular words come to mind?

2. Jesus made a bold symbolic statement at the wedding in
   Cana when he desecrated the holy water jars with party wine,
   thereby replacing ceremony with celebration. If Jesus came
   today, what sacred traditions or long-standing beliefs do you
   think he would need to challenge in order to make his point?

3. Notice that Jesus and his disciples were at the wedding party
   because they were "invited." If you were throwing a party,
   would you want Jesus to be there? Why or why not?

4. A close read of the text of John 2 reveals that the water turns
   into wine only when the servants actually follow Jesus' instructions to serve it. Jesus does not perform the miracle first by
   himself and then allow the servants to tell others about it.
   Rather, their participation becomes part of the transformation.
   Are there lessons in this for us?

---

*"The kingdom of heaven is like a king
who prepared a wedding banquet."*

— MATTHEW 22:2

CHAPTER TWO

Religion, Spirituality, and Faith

The revelation of God is the abolition of religion.
— KARL BARTH

Language is fluid. It changes shape as contexts and cultures change. For instance, we are living at a time when more and more people are making a distinction between religion and spirituality.[1]

By "religion" people tend to refer to established *systems* of belief about Ultimate Reality and the *institutions* that maintain them. I use the word *religion* in a similar way, to refer to "any reliance on systems or institutions, rules or rituals as our conduit to God." The "religion" I'm talking about in this book is any system of rules, regulations, rituals, and routines that people use to achieve their spiritual end-goal, their *telos*, whether they call that enlightenment, salvation, nirvana, union with the Divine, or something else. I don't believe that any one system or institution is the way to connect with God, although these things may be able to play a supportive role in our journey.[2]

When we talk this way, we are walking in the footsteps of great thinkers like the existential philosopher Søren Kierkegaard (who distinguished between the faith of Christianity and the religion of Christendom), Swiss theologian Karl Barth (who called the church back to a Christ-centered faith), and German theologian Dietrich Bonhoeffer. Bonhoeffer is a hero to many for standing up to the spineless religiosity of the German Lutheran Church during World War II. While in prison before his execution by the Nazis, Bonhoeffer wrote his *Letters and Papers from Prison*, in which he sets up the antinomy between faith and religion and argues passionately for a "nonreligious" or "religionless Christianity."

Religionless Christianity. I can picture Jesus smiling over that one.

The Jesus described in the Bible sees the things people normally associate with religion, like prayer and pilgrimage, baptism and Bible study, church attendance and charitable giving, as possible *expressions* of the spiritual life God gives, but not the means to obtain it. Do I kiss my wife to earn her love? Or do I kiss her to express the love that we already share? One represents the insecurity of religion. The other shows the intimacy of faith.

The good news message of Jesus is that God gives us spiritual life as a gift, which the biblical writers summarized by the word "grace." Sure, God wants us to live good lives, but the goodness we live out in this world is an act of gratitude for our spiritual life and not a religious attempt to be good enough to earn that life.

The earliest Christ-followers taught that living a good and loving life should be the joyful expression of a person who has received eternal life, salvation, as a gift (see Romans 6:23). We should not carry the burden of trying to live an exceptionally good life in order to be qualified for salvation. Christ-followers are encouraged in the New Testament to live a loving life out of gratitude, not out of fear of losing their spot in heaven. What kind of loving marriage would it be if I treated my wife kindly only out of fear that she would divorce me if I didn't? What kind of a son would I be if I honored my aging parents only because I wanted the reward of their inheritance? What kind of father would I be if I treated my children lovingly only because I was afraid that if I abused them, they would tattle on me? Rather, I show my love toward my family out of a sense of privilege and gratitude for our relationship and because their love has won my heart.

The apostle Paul often expresses this idea in his letters to the first generation of Christ-followers:

> God saved you by his grace when you believed. And you can't take credit for this; it is a gift from God. Salvation is not a reward for the good things we have done, so none of us can boast about it. For we are God's masterpiece. He has created us anew in Christ Jesus, so we can do the good things he planned for us long ago. (Ephesians 2:8-10, NLT)

Notice that the gift of spiritual life comes first. Then good works come as a result. This kind of good behavior is not like a prisoner's attempt to impress the warden in order to achieve early parole. Rather, it is the joyful and grateful expression of a prisoner unexpectedly set free. The motive is the *absence* of fear, not its *presence*. The apostle John wrote: "There is no fear in love, but perfect love casts out fear; for fear has to do with punishment, and whoever fears has not reached perfection in love" (1 John 4:18, NRSV).

This is the "easy" yoke of Jesus that we talked about in the preface. We do not have to work for salvation — whether those works are generic good deeds or expressly religious behaviors, such as prayer or Scripture study or other rituals. Instead, God gives us salvation, life, love, and everything we need up front, including a purpose in this world. It is his gift to us (see Romans 6:23). When we realize this down to the depth of our bones, we then naturally live a life that expresses our gratitude by loving God and others. To do otherwise would be false and forced.

Religious people miss this message and turn to the rituals and regulations, ethics and activities prescribed to them as the way to achieve what God has already offered them as a gift. In so doing, they miss the life of God and fail to satisfy their spiritual thirst.

Picture a thirsty person holding a cup of water. Now picture that person licking the outside of the cup in an attempt to quench his thirst. That is a picture of religion. Religious people tend to focus on the cup and forget about the contents. They argue about which cup is best, but forget to drink from any. Some cups are ornate and some are simple. People are attracted to different kinds, yet none of them will quench your thirst. I'm not saying there is no refreshment to be found within any one cup, only that the religion itself is not what refreshes. In fact, whenever we think we have found *the* cup, we should probably throw it away, because we have already confused the contents with the container, substance with structure, faith with form. Faith can be expressed in many forms, but the form is not what satisfies. The Bible calls this process of confusing form with substance "idolatry," and it happens to well-meaning people all the time.

The Bible tells a story about a time when God used a statue of a snake to help generate faith among his people. Poisonous snakes were attacking the Israelites and many were dying. They prayed to God to remove the snakes, but instead he came up with a more creative plan to rescue them.[3] He could have just healed everyone on his own, but as God typically does, he found a way to partner with his people to produce results. So God had Moses construct a snake statue and told the people that looking to the snake statue in faith would bring healing. The statue was God's idea, and it served its intended purpose well (see Numbers 21:4-9). Yet later in the Bible, we find that the people became so enamored with the statue of the serpent that they started worshipping *it* rather than the God who gave it to them (see 2 Kings 18:4). What was meant to be a gift from God had become an idol, a hindrance to their direct relationship with God. Instead of worshipping God, they were worshipping the form his power took at one point in their lives. They were licking the cup.

Sometimes people who know I am a Christ-follower ask me if I think all religions lead to God. I suppose they are waiting to see if I argue that only the Christian religion is the way to God or if I will give the open-minded answer that all religions lead to God. Instead I choose a third alternative. I tell them that I do not believe all religions lead to God because *no* religion leads to God. Religion does not lead people to

God any more than cups quench your thirst.

The story of the Bible is the story of God wanting us to come to him *directly*, offering us tools to help our relationship, and then watching broken-hearted as we fall in love with the tools, rather than God. Through the Hebrew prophet Jeremiah, God expresses his disappointment at our tendencies:

> "For My people have committed two evils:
> They have forsaken Me,
> The fountain of living waters,
> To hew for themselves cisterns,
> Broken cisterns
> That can hold no water." (Jeremiah 2:13, NASB)

God himself is the fountain of living water that quenches human thirst (also see Jeremiah 17:13). God does not say to his people, "Hey, listen, you've got it all wrong. You're drinking from the wrong cup. Choose the right cup and then you will please me!" No! The God of the Bible does not advocate for one right "cup" by which to experience his thirst-quenching love. Rather, *he invites us to come to him directly*, the fountain of living waters. And on top of that, when we refuse to come to him, *he* comes to *us*, offering to put his thirst-quenching Spirit inside us. That is the story of Jesus (see John 4:7-14; 7:37-39).

There are many Old Testament prophecies about the end of religion, and all of them take shape to some degree in the life of Jesus. For instance, the prophet Isaiah says:

> Forget the former things;
>   do not dwell on the past.
> See, I am doing a new thing!
>   Now it springs up; do you not perceive it?
> I am making a way in the wilderness
>   and streams in the wasteland. (Isaiah 43:18-19)

Are you noticing a liquid theme going on here? The Bible often compares God's Spirit to liquids like water, oil, milk, or wine. Jesus used this liquid imagery to proclaim the end of religion. Two other Hebrew prophets had foretold a time when "living water" would flow from the temple in Jerusalem to the rest of the land, bringing spiritual refreshment to all people (see Ezekiel 47:1-12; Zechariah 14:8-9). It was a vivid picture of global renewal. But how would that prophecy come to pass? What would this liquid prophecy look like when it happens in "real" life? Pictorial prophecies are notoriously difficult to interpret. Water bubbling up from underneath the temple and flowing outward to flood the dry and thirsty land. What did the vision mean? Would the entire world one day worship Israel's God by coming to the Jewish temple to offer animal sacrifices? Why does the prophecy picture the water flowing *from* the temple *to* all the world rather than portray people coming to the temple to drink?

Jesus believed in this prophecy, but he believed it would be fulfilled in a yet-unheard-of radical way. His subversive message to the religious people of his day was that he would replace the temple sacrificial system, and through him all the world could receive God's blessing *directly*. The life-giving water of the prophecies would flow out of *him*, the new temple. As we will see in greater detail in part 2, Jesus acted as though his own life and death replaced the entire temple sacrificial system. Jesus himself would take on the role of all three: the sacrificial lamb, the priest offering the sacrifice, and even the temple itself. Jesus believed the prophecy would come to pass and that "living water" would flow from the temple, but not like anyone could have anticipated. He was the new temple, and he would make it possible for all of us to become part of this new reality.

Jesus went public with this message in Jerusalem at a religious festival called the Feast of Tabernacles. One of the rituals at this multiday celebration involved a processional that carried water to the temple where it was poured over the altar as a symbolic offering. Taking advantage of this aquatic imagery, Jesus makes his move:

On the last and most important day of the festival, Jesus stood up and shouted, "If you are thirsty, come to me and drink! Have faith in me, and you will have life-giving water flowing from deep inside you, just as the Scriptures say." Jesus was talking about the Holy Spirit, who would be given to everyone that had faith in him. (John 7:37-39, CEV. Also see John 4:7-14.)

Notice that Jesus is not just adding on something new to the religion of his day. With this offer, he is supplanting it. Through Jesus, God would come and dwell within individuals, enlivening them with his refreshing presence from the inside out. No longer would the religious faithful need to commute to a special place to meet with God. Instead, God's Spirit would be with them, in them, and flow out from them through faith.

It may seem like Jesus is just replacing one intermediary between God and humanity (the temple) with another (himself). But that is only half the story. If Jesus really is God coming to us in the flesh—our theme for chapter 14—then Christ's words take on new significance. Through Jesus, God is saying that *God* is the way to God. In other words, God wants to relate to us directly, and so he has come directly to us in a form we can relate to.

Today, many people use the term "spirituality" the same way Jesus used the word "faith"—to describe the relationship one has with Ultimate Reality *directly*, above and beyond the systems and institutions of religion. Some religious people feel threatened by this kind of talk. Personally, I am encouraged, because I think we are finally catching up to what Jesus has been saying for over two thousand years.

The Jesus described in the Bible never uses the word *religion* to refer to what he came to establish, nor does he invite people to join a particular institution or organization. When he speaks of the "church," he is talking about the people who gather in his name, not the structure they meet in or the organization they belong to (see Matthew 18:15-20). And when he talks about connecting with God, he consistently speaks not of religion but of "faith" (Luke 7:50; John 3:14-16). Jesus never commands his followers to embrace detailed creeds or codes of conduct, and he never instructs his followers to participate in exhaustive religious rituals. His life's work was about undoing the knots that bound people to ritual and empty tradition.

At the same time, Jesus never taught that people could experience true spirituality simply by stopping those same religious rituals. Please understand—and this is important—becoming a religion dropout does not by itself make you more spiritual. Jesus taught that the secret was a change of heart, not a change of religious expression. He didn't just want people to stop licking the cup—he wanted them to drink!

I have met many people who call themselves spiritual as a way of saying that they just don't care to go to church or synagogue or mosque or temple anymore. But being spiritual is not about what you don't do. Yes, walking in the woods can be a spiritual experience, but it can also just be a walk in the woods. Likewise, going to church can be a spiritual experience, or it can just be a religious tradition. The heart of the matter is the human heart.

There is a difference, an important difference, between relating to God through systems of doctrines, codes of conduct, inherited traditions, or institutions of power, and relating to God directly, soul-to-soul, mind-to-mind, heart-to-heart. Jesus taught this distinction, lived this message, and was killed because of its implications.

In one scandalous scene recorded in John 4, Jesus initiates a conversation with a Samaritan woman with a disgraceful reputation. The fact he even has this conversation challenges multiple religious boundaries. First of all, he is talking with a Samaritan (ethnic and religious enemies of the first-century Jews). Secondly, he is striking up a conversation with a woman (in a day when religious leaders taught that a man should never talk to a woman in public, not even his own wife!). Thirdly, he is interacting with a known "sinner," a sexually broken woman with a bad reputation. To this unlikely person Jesus unveils God's plan for humankind—to inaugurate a new way of communing directly with himself.

In their conversation, the woman raises the subject of an ongoing religious debate between Jews and Samaritans: Which holy mountain should God be worshipped on? It is a debate that lives on today in the my-religion-is-better-than-your-religion attitude of so many religious people. Jesus responds with words supersaturated with irreligious connotations:

> Jesus replied, "Believe me, dear woman, the time is coming when it will no longer matter whether you worship the Father on this mountain or in Jerusalem. . . . But the time is coming—indeed it's here now—when true worshipers will worship the Father in spirit and in truth. The Father is looking for those who will worship him that way. For God is Spirit, so those who worship him must worship in spirit and in truth." (John 4:21,23-24, NLT)

This time of pure spiritual connection with the Divine is not only "coming" but is "here now," says Jesus. The very presence of Jesus changes the Jewish messianic concept of *anticipation* of God's kingdom on earth to a disposition of *realization*. And what is to be realized now? What does Jesus say he is inaugurating with his coming? A spirituality that transcends any one religious system.

The spirituality—the faith—that Jesus came to bring is not dependant upon place or procedure, but on an inside-out relationship with God. God is beyond any one temple or any one race, and those who will worship him acceptably must embrace this reality (more on this concept in part 2). The key to overcoming religious barriers that prevent unity is to do away with religion as our primary source of identity altogether. The external forms become meaningless when we embrace and cultivate an inner parent-child relationship of love between God and us. God is not just the Ruler of a cosmos; he is the Father of a family. Jesus dared this woman to cross the borders of her physically focused religion into his spiritual family. I think he offers us the same invitation today.

Few things take more courage and humility than to rethink one's worldview. To the extent we have established our identity in a specific framework, questioning it can feel like we are losing our sense of self. Perhaps this is why Jesus spoke of the need to be "born again" to a religious man entrenched in his own worldview (see John 3:1-8).[4] Yes, we may grieve the loss of our old identity, but there is new life on the other side of this process of personal death and resurrection.

I am one of the growing number of people whose lives have been touched by the irreligious spirituality of the rabbi from Nazareth. At the same time, I am deeply saddened and sometimes angered by the variety of ways his teaching and example have been codified, conceptualized, and institutionalized by a religion that bears his name but all too often misses his message.

I am convinced that, rightly understood and fully embraced, the message of Jesus can transform our lives in a way no religion ever could. So, when someone says to me, "I'm spiritual but not religious," I imagine Jesus sighing with relief.

At the same time, becoming a spiritual person, or person of faith, should never be an end in itself. Our goal should not be to simply "have faith" or "be spiritual," as though these ideals are worth pursuing in and of themselves. Faith and spirituality are connecting concepts—they describe the connection we can have with something or someone beyond and within ourselves. Our world is full of people who say "I'm a spiritual person" as though spirituality is their goal, that thing they have been looking for all their lives. They are like people who describe themselves as "romantic" on Internet dating sites, but who never have anyone in their lives to be romantic with. Their "romance" is just a hollow ideal without a relationship within which to express it. Just because we cry when watching movies or reading novels doesn't mean we are romantic; it means we're sentimental. And just because we don't like religion doesn't mean we are spiritual. The question is, *Who* are you spiritual *with*?

Faith, likewise, is about two people engaging in a trust-based relationship. Faith functions in a human life like a window functions in a home. A window is not something you hang on a wall to be looked *at* like a picture, but a space to be looked *through* at the beauty outside. A window is not beautiful in itself, and staring *at* one without looking *through* it misses the point. Likewise, faith in and of itself is never the end goal. I don't think of myself as "a person of faith" but as a follower of Christ—and that act takes faith.

Abraham Joshua Heschel reflects this sentiment when he writes,

The issue of prayer is not prayer;
the issue of prayer is God.[5]

Faith, like prayer, should be a way of connecting with God. I have talked with many spiritually seeking people who are struggling to find satisfaction because they are using the window of faith more like a mirror. They have caught sight of their own reflection in the window glass and have forgotten to adjust their depth of focus, to look beyond themselves to see the beauty that surrounds them—the beauty that is God. Today there are many books, seminars, and courses available that will only encourage this tendency to use the window of spirituality more like a mirror, and many of them are very popular. After all, aren't *we* our own favorite subjects? But faith is too precious to be cheapened by narcissism.

So if you consider yourself a spiritual person, let me offer one word of advice early in this book. Use the window of faith to look beyond yourself. Adjust your depth of focus. Look *through* the window. Other devices besides spirituality can function as better mirrors, if that is what you are looking for. But if you are reading this book, I trust that you are searching for something more than a mere reflection. Hey, you look good. Your hair is fine, and there is nothing caught in your teeth. Now let's stop staring at ourselves and look *through* the window to see what is out there.

Q & Eн?

1. Like the word *trunk*, people use the word *religion* to mean different things. For the purposes of this book, I am using the word *religion* to refer to "reliance on systems or institutions as our conduit to God," whereas I am using the word *spirituality* to refer to "a direct connection with the Divine," summed up in Jesus' use of the word *faith*—a relational word meaning "trust."

   - What, if any, has been your experience with religion?
   - What, if any, has been your experience with spirituality?
   - What, if any, has been your experience with Jesus?

2. In what ways have you observed people "licking the cup" in our world today?

3. Jesus says in John 4 that God wants people to worship him "in spirit and in truth" (4:24). What do you think each of these qualities is describing?

4. Do an honest self-assessment. How fixated do you tend to be on "cup" issues? It can happen in two ways:

   - Do your attitudes show that you tend to lick any one cup for spiritual refreshment?
   - Or do you tend to reject all cups, throwing them aside in an effort to be nonreligious, and miss out on the value of their contents in the process?

5. More self-assessment. Can you think of ways that you tend to use faith and spirituality as mirrors instead of windows?

Yet a time is coming and has now come when the true worshipers will worship the Father in the Spirit and in truth, for they are the kind of worshipers the Father seeks.

— JOHN 4:23

CHAPTER THREE

Blue Rose Tuesdays

All you need is love.
— THE BEATLES

Jesus often taught through stories of everyday life called parables, and now it's my turn. So gather around, boys and girls. It's story time with Uncle Brux.

Bob and Sue Prunebottom were a few years into their marriage when Sue felt the need to challenge Bob on the lack of romance they were experiencing. Gone were the days when he had initiated exciting and unexpected events that brought the two of them together romantically. Now their marriage consisted of a steady diet of predictable rituals and routines that maintained stability but lacked passion. This was, understandably, not enough for Sue. Bob agreed and committed to taking the initiative to help rekindle some of the former romance they had shared together.

One Tuesday evening, around six thirty, the doorbell rang: *ding, dong*. Sue went to the door to find little Maureen Tupperman, their usual babysitter. Sue was surprised since she knew she hadn't booked Maureen, and she was even more surprised when Maureen explained: "*Mr.* Prunebottom booked me." Now this was a first. *Bob* had called the babysitter all on his own?

Sure enough, Bob came to the door, welcomed in little Maureen, and asked Sue to head upstairs and put on whatever she would enjoy wearing out on the town. Wow. Romance was returning.

Sue came down minutes later in a beautiful red dress and off they drove together. They pulled into the parking lot of a fancy little Italian restaurant. As they walked in the front door, they were cheerfully greeted by the manager. "Your table is all ready, Mr. Prunebottom," he said with a knowing smile. Then he led the couple to a charming, candle-lit table for two in the back corner of the restaurant. Waiting for Sue at her place setting was a card with her name on it. She opened it up to see something beautiful. It wasn't the usual Hallmark special with a prefab message and Bob's signature. It was a simple card with no factory message on the inside, but a deeply thoughtful, handwritten note from Bob about his love for—and delight with—Sue.

As the evening progressed, Bob and Sue enjoyed a truly meaningful conversation over candlelight and wine. When the dessert came, Bob reached under the table and pulled out Sue's favorite flower—a single, stunning blue rose. His thoughtfulness down to the last detail was a precious gift to Sue, and she was moved to tears.

That week was one of the most wonderful weeks of their married life. Bob's intentionality, mindfulness, and creative initiative filled Sue with renewed hope for the future. And Bob was feeling like he had become the husband he always wanted to be. "How can I make this last?" Bob wondered.

The next Tuesday night, at exactly six thirty, the doorbell rang: *ding, dong.* Sure enough it was young Maureen Tupperman. Sue was again taken aback, especially when she learned that Mr. Prunebottom had made the arrangements *again. Two weeks in a row!* thought Sue. *I could get used to this!*

She did think it was a bit odd when Bob encouraged her to put on that same red dress that she wore the previous week, but gladly made herself ready for another night out together. As they pulled into the parking lot of the same little Italian restaurant, Sue thought to herself that Bob might not get full marks for creativity this time, but a night out was a night out, and she would be happy with their evening together. She was again touched to find a card waiting for her at the same table at the back of the restaurant. But her delight turned to disappointment when she saw that Bob had written almost exactly the same words on the inside. Now the evening was beginning to feel not romantic but just plain weird. Refusing to draw attention to Bob's lack of creativity, Sue determined to enjoy the night. Bob ordered them the exact same meal as the week previous, and as the evening moved forward Sue became aware of how he manipulated their conversation to cover basically the same relational territory as the week before. Now Sue could almost hear the *Twilight Zone* theme playing in the back of her mind. Whenever she tried to take their conversation in a new direction, Bob seemed to find a way to bring it back to the same issues, the same questions, even the same jokes that passed between them the former Tuesday. For Sue, the evening went from feeling weird to feeling suffocating. A part of her wanted out, yet another part of her wanted to give Bob every benefit of the doubt. Perhaps the joke would soon end. It came as no surprise that when dessert arrived Bob reached under the table and pulled out—you guessed it—a single blue rose. Sue received it with polite gratitude, but the tears that welled up in her eyes this night were for a different reason.

Bob and Sue enjoyed a cordial but mildly distant relationship that week, until the following Tuesday evening, at six thirty, when Sue heard: *ding, dong.* Once again, Bob manipulated Sue through a scripted evening of supposed romance. Very little was different from the previous two Tuesdays. Now Sue was plainly discouraged. Visions of Bill Murray's *Groundhog Day* kept coming to mind. Sure enough, the following Tuesday at six thirty: *ding, dong.* And a week later: *ding, dong.* And so on, and so forth, Tuesday after Tuesday, blue rose after blue rose.

And today, if you were to ask Bob how his marriage is doing, he would probably smile with a sense of accomplishment and say, "I romance my wife religiously." He might even boast about finding the secret to a successful relationship and encourage you to follow his system for a healthy marriage.

If you were to ask Sue how things are going, you know you would get a different take on things. Most likely, she would burst into tears and then tell you she feels trapped, imprisoned in a loveless relationship by someone who means well, but who doesn't have a sweet clue what relationship is all about. And me, I'm left wondering if this is how God feels sometimes.

Bob mistook the *form* for the *substance*. He turned their *relationship* into a kind of *religion*. He lost the *heart* of his connection with his wife. The fact is, after months of Bob's dinner routine, Sue could have been dining with anyone who had memorized their dating traditions. Love was unnecessary. The system Bob created allowed him to function on autopilot.

This illustrates why Jesus always—ALWAYS—puts the emphasis of his teaching on heart issues, not behavioral routines. If the heart is right, loving actions will follow.

For instance, Jesus is not content with people following the commandment "Thou shalt not kill." Instead, he points out that a person could go his entire life avoiding murder and still have a heart filled with hate rather than love. Deal with the heart issue, and not only will people not murder each other, but they will actually *love* one another (see Matthew 5:17-48). Jesus' goal for his followers is never just a life without obvious sin, but a life filled with genuine love.

Routines. Rituals. Customs. Traditions. They can be used to enhance or to kill intimacy. Over time, intentional thoughtfulness can be lost since the routines do all the thinking for us. We are left with something that looks good on the outside, but is filled with nothing but the bones of a long-dead relationship. This is true of any romantic relationship, including our relationship with God. Jesus criticizes the religious leaders of his day for this very thing: "How terrible for you, teachers of the Law and Pharisees! You hypocrites! You are like white-washed tombs, which look fine on the outside but are full of bones and decaying corpses on the inside" (Matthew 23:27, TEV).

Ouch. That's gonna leave a mark.

Don't get me wrong. Many couples weave a wonderful romantic routine into the rhythm of their relationship, and so find themselves enjoying the regularity of what had become death for Bob and Sue's relationship. Another couple might eat at the same restaurant regularly because they first met there and the atmosphere reminds them of their romantic history. For them, the regularity enhances their intimacy, the form complements the substance of their relationship. There is nothing intrinsically wrong with the pattern. But when the pattern is all you are left with, the love is gone. So it is with all religious tradition.

We must remember that the enemy is not tradition itself, but the complete dependence upon tradition and routine to the point where we disengage from thoughtful, purposeful, intentional intimacy. God hates it when that happens. More than once in the Bible, when Israel continued their religious traditions but forgot the heart of it all, he told them so.

"I hate, I despise your religious festivals;
    I cannot stand your assemblies.
Even though you bring me burnt offerings and grain offerings,
    I will not accept them.
Though you bring choice fellowship offerings,
    I will have no regard for them.
Away with the noise of your songs!
    I will not listen to the music of your harps.
But let justice roll on like a river,
    righteousness like a never-failing stream!" (Amos 5:21-24; also
        see Isaiah 1:10-18)

Surely these words are just as applicable to the Christian church. In chapter 4, we will take a look at the ugliness of church history when Christians make the same mistake, going through the religious motions but forgetting the heart of Christ in the middle of it all. And in the background, you just might hear the echo of God's voice in the above passage: *I hate, I despise your religious routines when you fail to live out your faith in the totality of your lives.*

Q & Eн?

1. What is your reaction to the "parable" in this chapter? Do you see yourself in it? Do you see God in it?

2. If we see a couple in the same restaurant each week, can we judge them for having lost the love in their relationship? Likewise, if we know of people who participate in daily or weekly routines or traditions to enhance their spiritual life, can we judge them for being too religious?

3. How do you think traditions and routines can

   • help us develop our spiritual lives? Use examples.
   • hinder our spiritual growth? Use examples.

———◆+✕+◆———

"You're hopeless, you religion scholars and Pharisees! Frauds! You burnish the surface of your cups and bowls so they sparkle in the sun, while the insides are maggoty with your greed and gluttony. Stupid Pharisee! Scour the insides, and then the gleaming surface will mean something."

— MATTHEW 23:25-26, MSG

———◆+✕+◆———

CHAPTER FOUR

Chamber of Horrors

*I don't reject your Christ, I love your Christ. It's just that so many
of you Christians are so unlike your Christ.*

— GANDHI

If the history of religion were turned into a series of displays in a wax
museum, visitors might think they had entered the Chamber of Horrors.
A centerpiece of the museum would be a body lurching toward you,
seemingly animated—but headless. The descriptive plaque would read,
"The institutional church throughout much of its history."

The early disciples of Jesus thought of themselves as intimately
connected with Christ, like a body to its head (see Romans 12:4-5; 1
Corinthians 12:12-14; Ephesians 4:15-16; Colossians 2:19). Jesus, as the
head of the body of Christ, was the leader, the one who made the decisions. He called his followers to live radical lives of active peacemaking,
courageous nonviolence, limitless forgiveness, and other-centered love
(see Matthew 5:38-47; Luke 6:27-36). Yet over time, the institutional
church seems to have been severed from its head, and as a result became
one of the most violent religions in history.

My wife, Nina, and I recently had dinner in the home of a passionate atheist whose vehement disdain for the Christian religion was
obvious from the beginning of the evening. He brought his prized
multivolume encyclopedia of Christian horrors to the dining room and
dropped them on the table with a dramatic thud. The books offered a
detailed tour through church history; grim facts that probably are not

highlighted in many Bible school texts. My dinner host, obviously well prepared for this moment, challenged me: "Didn't Jesus say we could know a tree by its fruit?"

"Yes," I agreed. He was referring to places in the Bible where Jesus uses the analogy of good and bad fruit to warn about false prophets and spiritual fakers, saying things like:

> "By their fruit you will recognize them. Do people pick grapes from thornbushes, or figs from thistles? Likewise, every good tree bears good fruit, but a bad tree bears bad fruit. A good tree cannot bear bad fruit, and a bad tree cannot bear good fruit. Every tree that does not bear good fruit is cut down and thrown into the fire. Thus, by their fruit you will recognize them." (Matthew 7:16-20)

"Well, then, isn't it conclusive?" he continued, with a hand on the books. "The tree begun by Jesus bears so much bad fruit! By Jesus' own words, the way of Jesus *must* be rejected."

I thought my dinner host had a great point. We should put the history of the Christian religion to the very test that Jesus advocated — test the fruit to see if it is good. Of course, my host's point was that, if we consider church history to be the fruit of Jesus' teaching, then using Jesus' own test, we should consider the "tree" of Jesus' teaching bad. I disagreed with that implication, for reasons I will share in a moment, but the exercise seemed worthwhile.

I am aware that Christians are responsible for many wonderful examples of charity and benevolence through the centuries.[1] But these positive examples cannot nor should not undo the repulsive effects of the judgmental bigotry and horrific violence that permeates church history. The history of the Christian religion is like sweet-tasting fruit infested with worms. How can someone appreciate the sweetness of the fruit when they have just bitten into a worm? It does no good to remind them how delicious the fruit tastes. The worms spoil everything.[2]

So let us have the courage to pose the question: If, according to Jesus, we can recognize a tree by its fruit, and if church history is the fruit of Jesus' teaching, then should we not reject Jesus as the bad tree that has produced bad fruit? We will explore this issue more in pages to come, but for now let me tell you what I told my host that evening.

The history of the church is not an example of Jesus' teaching bearing bad fruit, but of his teaching being completely ignored, rationalized, or trivialized—and *that* bearing bad fruit. Most people who are hostile toward Christianity realize that Jesus is not to blame. In fact, they rightly judge and condemn Christians in terms of what Jesus taught.

The challenge for all would-be Christ-followers today is to participate in the grand experiment of actually living out the simple way of peace as taught and exemplified by Jesus in the Bible. If masses of people who claim to be Christians actually began to live like Christ, think of how luscious that fruit would be. To paraphrase G. K. Chesterton—the way of Jesus has not been tried and found unfruitful. It has been found difficult, and left untried.

In his book *The Great Omission* Dallas Willard uses an automotive illustration to make a similar point:

> If your neighbor is having trouble with his automobile, you might think he just got a lemon. And you might be right. But if you found that he was supplementing his gasoline with a quart of water now and then, you would not blame the car or its maker for it not running, or for running in fits and starts. You would say that the car was not built to work under the conditions imposed by the owner. And you would certainly advise him to put only the appropriate kind of fuel in the tank. After restorative work, perhaps the car would then run fine.[3]

Before we blame Jesus for offering us a lemon of a religion, we should examine whether the blame lies more with the Christian church for "watering down" Christ's message. Perhaps the problem is not with

Jesus' teaching, but with Christians' simply not doing what he said.

So now let's take the time to look into the abyss that my dinner host focused on. Certainly we must agree with N. T. Wright's understatement, that "Christianity has been responsible for many great evils."[4] Perhaps if we stare long and hard at some of the worms in the apple of Christianity, we can better discern how they got in there, what their effect has been, and what we should do about this rotting apple of religion.

Have you ever noticed that wax museums usually have a detour that allows squeamish customers to skip the Chamber of Horrors section? So right here, right now—this is your detour sign. Feel free to flip ahead whenever you feel your stomach getting woozy.

For those of you with the resolve to read on, remember that we are talking about a religion that was supposedly founded on the teachings of a man undeniably dedicated to radical *non*violence; a man who was prophesied to be the "Prince of Peace" (Isaiah 9:6).

The Crusades. In 1095 Pope Urban II called for the knights of Europe to unite and march to Jerusalem to save the Holy Land from the rule of the Islamic infidels. Just decades earlier, Pope Gregory VII had declared, "Cursed be the man who holds back his sword from shedding blood," and now his wishes were coming to pass. The Crusaders rode into battle with the cry *Deus volt*—"God wills it!" Raymond of Agiles accompanied the Crusaders as a representative of the church during the first Crusade. He documented the taking of Jerusalem with these words:

> Wonderful things were to be seen. Numbers of Saracens
> (Muslims) were beheaded. . . . Others were shot with arrows,
> or forced to jump from the towers; others were tortured for sev-
> eral days, then burned with flames. Piles of heads, hands, and
> feet were to be seen in the streets of the city. It was necessary
> to pick one's way over the bodies of men and horses. But these
> were small matters compared to what happened at the temple
> of Solomon. . . . What happened there? If I tell the truth, it will

exceed your powers of belief. So let it suffice to say this much at least, that in the temple and portico of Solomon, men rode in blood up to their knees and the bridle reins. Indeed, it was a just and splendid judgment of God, that this place should be filled with the blood of the unbelievers, when it had suffered so long from their blasphemies.[5]

Men, women, and children—Muslim and Jewish—all slaughtered in the name of Jesus. The synagogue in which the city's Jews were sheltering was set on fire to burn them alive. At the end of the day's brutality, Crusaders gathered "full of happiness and weeping for joy," for a time of worship in the Church of the Holy Sepulcher.[6]

If this book were a screenplay, at this point (and throughout the rest of this chapter) I would suggest inserting flashback scenes to Jesus' words on the subject of enemy-love and nonviolence.

"This is what I say to all who will listen to me:

"Love your enemies, and be good to everyone who hates you. Ask God to bless anyone who curses you, and pray for everyone who is cruel to you. If someone slaps you on one cheek, don't stop that person from slapping you on the other cheek. If someone wants to take your coat, don't try to keep back your shirt. Give to everyone who asks and don't ask people to return what they have taken from you. Treat others just as you want to be treated.

"If you love only someone who loves you, will God praise you for that? Even sinners love people who love them. If you are kind only to someone who is kind to you, will God be pleased with you for that? Even sinners are kind to people who are kind to them." (Luke 6:27-33, CEV)

Let the words you have just read ring in your ears as you read on. Unfortunately, many who have claimed to be followers of Jesus seem to have demonstrated an acute case of selective hearing. Church history reveals that Jesus' message of enemy-love and nonviolent peacemaking was deeply needed but rarely heeded.

End of flashback.

Although other crusades would be launched against Muslims (and any Jews who happened to be in the way), many church-motivated killing sprees were specifically directed against Jews. After all, hadn't the Jews killed Christ? Church leaders missed the point of the Passion narratives, which serve as an indictment against the blind religious leaders, not the Jewish people as a whole. And that same rebuke is transferable to the church! The church leaders ignored the fact that the New Testament's prosecution of religious hypocrisy must be applied to Christian leaders as much as any Jewish leaders in Jesus' day.

Besides killing people of other religions, the church sponsored crusades against any groups who claimed to be Christian but did not conform to standard church doctrine and practice, such as the Cathars.

Although unorthodox by Christian standards (and unattractive by my standards—hey, the leaders of this group didn't believe in having sex, eating meat, or drinking wine!), the Albigensians, or Cathars, were a pacifist movement, trying to live out many of the spiritual teachings of Jesus. In 1179 Pope Alexander III proclaimed a crusade against these peaceful Jesus-lovers. He promised two years indulgence (freedom from punishment for sins) to all who would take up arms, and eternal salvation for all who died in battle. The Pope's promises were not enough motivation to rally people in sufficient numbers against the popular Cathars. Yet in 1208, when Pope Innocent III offered, in addition to the indulgences and eternal salvation, the lands and property of the heretics and their supporters to any who would take up arms, the Cathar Crusade (also known as the Albigensian Crusade) swept through southern France.[7] "Anyone who attempts to construe a personal view of God which conflicts with Church dogma must be burned without pity," said Innocent III.[8] And so they were.

Over a thirty-year period, everyone associated with this sect was rounded up and slaughtered: men, women, and children. The entire population of the town of Béziers was slaughtered by Crusaders when the citizens refused to identify and hand over any known Cathars. Béziers is believed to have held just over two hundred Cathars, but ten thousand to twenty thousand citizens were killed.[9] Many people took refuge within the Cathedral of St. Nazaire, praying for divine intervention. The Crusaders broke in and, while singing hymns, slaughtered all the men, women, children, and infants. When some Crusaders asked the church leadership how they were to distinguish Catholic from Cathar, the commanding abbot, Arnaud-Amaury, is reported to have said the infamous line, *"Caedite eos! Novit enim Dominus qui sunt eius"* — Latin for "Slay them all! God will know his own." The Pope was kept fully informed of events. He seemed to glory in the violence, starting one letter to the front lines with: "Praise and thanks to the Lord for that which He hath wrought through thee . . . against His most penitential enemies."[10]

By the time it was over, the Cathar Crusade killed an estimated one million people, not only Cathars but much of the population of southern France. Its only motivation, according to the Catholic church, was the fight for religious purity.

The Inquisition. Pope Gregory IX launched the Monastic Inquisition in 1231, establishing priests of the Dominican order as a separate tribunal to root out heresy, accountable only to the Pope himself. In 1252, Pope Innocent IV sanctioned the use of torture in the pursuit of a confession from suspected heretics. The result was one of the most horrific realities our planet has ever seen — systematized torture, all in the name of Jesus. With license from the Pope himself, the supposed representative of Christ on earth, inquisitors were free to explore the depths of terror and cruelty.

Because the church believed that religious leaders should never spill blood, new methods of torture were invented to aid the hypocrisy. The rack, the hoist, thumbscrews, and water tortures were among the most common. Christian leaders also devised numerous other kinds of torture involving slowly dislocating or dismembering the body. Pincers had to be white hot so that the heated metal would cauterize the wound as the flesh was being torn open. Many of the torture devices used by the Inquisition were inscribed with the motto "Glory be only to God."

This was not just a brief moment in time. The Inquisition and its church-sponsored terror lasted for centuries. Most of the damage of the Inquisition was done during its earlier years under the direction of the Grand Inquisitor, Tomás de Torquemada, but for centuries, a few people every year continued to be burned alive as an *auto da fe* ("act of faith"). The last victim of the Inquisition, a schoolteacher charged with heresy, was executed by strangulation in 1824.

Sometimes Protestants smugly emphasize the misdeeds of the Catholic Church. But when it came to killing heretics, even respected Reformers like John Calvin approved of their deaths.[11]

Witch Hunts. Catholics and Protestants both sought the death of suspected witches. Anyone who appeared to draw power from nature through herbs, who healed in unconventional ways, or who just happened to be in the wrong place at the wrong time could be accused of being a witch. Taking the Old Testament Law as their guide, Christians believed that death was the only option for anyone involved in sorcery (see Exodus 22:18), and so once arrested, people accused of witchcraft were rarely given any sentence but death.

Although men were also charged with witchcraft, women were the prime target of this accusation. Suspected witches could be held accountable for virtually every problem, whether personal misfortune, bad harvest, famine, or plague. Eventually, identified witches (who were almost always misidentified Christians) became the new scapegoats—a role formerly held by Jews.

Modern historians differ widely in their estimations of how many people were accused, tortured, and eventually killed as witches. Most guesses fall anywhere between sixty thousand and two hundred thousand suspected witches tortured and killed during "the burning times."[12] I once met a Christian who argued strongly for the lesser number, as though there was great purpose in exposing the exaggerations made by secular people regarding the failures of the church. I responded that killing sixty thousand people in the name of the love of Jesus is sixty thousand too many and that she was focused on the wrong argument. The real problem Christians need to face is not the exaggerated criticism of secular people, but the mind-blowing extent of the church's failure to follow Jesus.

I sometimes imagine what it might have been like to live in these earlier years. I think of my daughters being accused of witchcraft by someone who didn't like them and where that horrible suspicion might lead. I wonder how I could continue to call myself a "Christian" when the spiritual leaders I trusted and the institution I supported tortured and killed my kids, all in the name of Jesus. When I take the time to make it personal like this in my mind's eye, then I know that I stand on the side of Jesus and not on the side of the religion that bears his name. And I am left asking: Are the attitudes that led to these horrors gone? Or have they just gone underground?

Because she was not raised in a Christian home as I was, my wife has the advantage of seeing Christian culture in North America with a higher degree of objectivity. Often, when I'm listening to a televangelist or radio preacher (yes, I actually do that sometimes!), Nina asks, "Why is he so angry?" Because I was raised in the subculture of North American evangelicalism I am usually not aware of what is painfully obvious to her. So Nina helps me really hear the underlying anger this way: She tells me to listen to the tone of his voice, but at the same time imagine that he is talking about any topic other than Jesus. "What would you say if a professor was giving a lecture on biology with that tone of voice? Or if a commercial was describing the merits of a product? Or, even better, what would you say if a friend was talking about his or her new love interest this way? What would you think about their tone of voice then?" When I listen this way, a light goes on. Many Christian leaders and teachers seem to have an undercurrent of anger. This is so prevalent that it has become part of the evangelical Christian subculture in North America, leaving many Christians blind to the hostility this subculture projects.

Infighting. I know of a scene in a horror/comedy movie where a man's hand—just his hand—becomes possessed by an evil spirit. While being attacked by his own hand, the man hears his hand taunt him with mocking laughter (how a hand can make laughing sounds, I have no idea). The scene is bizarre. The audience wonders: *Is this man's hand really possessed, or is his mind playing tricks on him?* Either way, the man seems confident that he must take drastic action to defend himself. He cuts off his own hand, crying triumphantly, "Who's laughing now?"

I said earlier that a decapitated body would make an accurate picture of the church, the body of Christ. Allow me to take it one step further. To be more accurate, perhaps our waxwork body should be fully dismembered and lying as separate pieces. For centuries, Christians have often followed a repeated pattern of debate, divide, and fight; debate, divide, and fight. Debate theology, separate from those you can't convince, and then fight against all who disagree with you—whether with words or with swords. Catholic against Orthodox, Protestant against Catholic, and all against Anabaptists. I'm told there are over three thousand different Christian denominations on the planet as I write this book, and most of them had their genesis in an inability to stay unified in the face of differing opinions. *Religious people are notorious for confusing acceptance with agreement.* When that happens, people assume that disagreement must result in rejection and condemnation.

In AD 325, when Constantine called all Christian bishops to attend the Council of Nicaea, 250 attended that event in good faith, as brothers in Christ. They may have had differing opinions about a variety of theological issues, but for the most part, they at least considered each other fellow Christians, committed followers of Jesus. Discussions over their disagreements were in-house events, debates among committed family members. By the end of the Council of Nicaea, with the drawing up of the official creed (the Nicene Creed), the group of formerly united-although-diverse Christ-followers could now be officially divided into "orthodox" and "heretics," with the heretics being given the option of exile or death. Can the making of creeds and the arguing of theology be the basis for Christian unity?[13]

In his book *Christianity Is Not Religion*, James A. Fowler chastises the historical church for missing the mark:

> Christianity is not essentially assent to or belief in tenets of truth, but rather receptivity to and participation in the activity of the Being of the One who is Truth (John 14:6). Jesus did not say, "I came that you might have orthodox beliefs and defend them apologetically." He said, "I came that you might have life (the very Being of God) and have such more abundantly (in the abundant expression of God's character in our behavior)." (John 10:10)[14]

What would church history look like if people who claimed to follow Jesus actually tried to live out the *character* of Christ? Perhaps then the prayer of Jesus for the unity of his future followers would not be so sad to read:

> "I am praying not only for these disciples but also for all who will ever believe in me through their message. I pray that they will all be one, just as you and I are one—as you are in me, Father, and I am in you. And may they be in us so that the world will believe you sent me.
>
> "I have given them the glory you gave me, so they may be one, as we are one. I am in them and you are in me. May they experience such perfect unity that the world will know that you sent me and that you love them as much as you love me." (John 17:20-23, NLT)

Whenever I am feeling discouraged in my own relationship with God, I remember that even Jesus knows what it is like to have his prayers go unanswered. "It may sound strange to say," writes Brian McLaren, "but I feel sorry for Jesus, sorry for the way we've dumbed down, domesticated, regimented, or even ruined what he started."[15] I think philosopher Roy Clouser speaks for many of us when he says, "The history of religious institutions has been such an abysmal panorama of bigotry, persecution and cruelty that I can see why it could lead someone to wish to be rid of the whole business."[16]

It would be nice to comfort ourselves with thoughts of how much the Christian religion has progressed from the violent times discussed in this chapter, but that would be a false comfort. It is my conviction that many conservative Christian groups refrain from killing, not because they have matured, but because the institutional church has lost the power it once had. Violent attitudes may be muted in today's world, but they find ways to reemerge in different forms. Listen to the sermons and sound bites of many popular Christian leaders today and you will notice the same aggressive, angry, and uncharitable attitudes lingering beneath the surface.[17]

Western Christians often pour their energies into national politics as a way of clamoring for the power they once had in society. But history bears this out: Whenever the church gets into bed with political powers, the church becomes the state's whore.

Remember, none of this is the way of Jesus—it is the way of a movement that has lost its way and forgotten its own teachings. As the saying goes, "When all else fails, read the instructions."

Q & Eh?

1. What is your emotional experience reading this chapter?

2. What do you think has been God's emotional experience witnessing firsthand the history this chapter describes?

3. In what ways do you think the Christian church has
   (a) repented and radically changed from its violent past, and
   (b) maintained a similar attitude, even if the violence is muted
   in our contemporary world?

4. Read Matthew 5:38-47 and Luke 6:27-36 (if you don't have
   a Bible handy, Luke 6:27-36 is quoted in this chapter). Also,
   think of what you know about how Jesus lived his life and
   how he died. If Jesus wanted his followers to be committed to
   the path of nonviolent resolution of conflict, is there anything
   more he could have said or done to be clear?

5. Why do you think Christians have such a hard time following
   Christ?

6. Who do you think were more "Christian" — the theologically
   "orthodox" Crusaders or the "heretical" but pacifist Cathars?

Do not repay anyone evil for evil, but take thought for what is noble in the sight of all. If it is possible, so far as it depends on you, live peaceably with all. Beloved, never avenge yourselves, but leave room for the wrath of God; for it is written, "Vengeance is mine, I will repay, says the Lord." No, "if your enemies are hungry, feed them; if they are thirsty, give them something to drink; for by doing this you will heap burning coals on their heads." Do not be overcome by evil, but overcome evil with good.

— ROMANS 12:17-21, NRSV

CHAPTER FIVE

Taking the "Mental" out of Fundamentalism

Our encouragement and call to Muslims to enter Jihad against
the American and the Israeli occupiers are actions which we are
engaging in as religious obligation.

— OSAMA BIN LADEN

Most religions contain two basic subgroups within their circle of faith: liberals and conservatives, or *moderates* and *fundamentalists*. Which group do you feel safer around?

Moderates are people who want to avoid the dangers and divisiveness of religious fundamentalism without leaving their religious heritage behind completely. Christian moderates, for instance, may attend church and read their Bible, but they always temper what they learn with the voice of reason, culture, and progress. Their goal is to avoid going overboard with the whole religion thing, to give it a place in their lives without allowing it to take over. Moderates of all religions usually get along better with nonbelievers, but they do not have the respect of the fundamentalists within their own faith.

Fundamentalists are those who call for a passionate return to the literal and authoritative teachings of their holy book, whatever that may be. When the holy book calls the faithful to "make war on the unbelievers" (9:73) and "slay the Pagans wherever you find them" (9:5), as does the Qur'an, or to stone your own children if they choose a differing religion, as does the Torah (Deuteronomy 13:6-11), we have a problem.

Moderates often feel like they have a role to play in helping fundamentalists see the destructive pattern to their overzealous commitment. But there is a problem with this approach. The moderate position cannot overcome what is perceived as an underlying weakness—moderates are not viewed by fundamentalists as completely faithful to their own texts. From a fundamentalist perspective, moderates have a divided allegiance. They are partially committed to their religion and partially to post-Enlightenment, secularized thinking. Fundamentalists believe moderates have arrived at their "soft" position, not because they have discovered it within their own sacred texts, but as a result of secular knowledge and selective scriptural neglect. This may result in a more articulate and gracious believer, but fundamentalists of the same faith will never take them seriously. Fundamentalists perceive moderates as halfhearted sellouts, which invalidates whatever meaningful critique moderates might offer fundamentalist religion. If fundamentalists are ever going to be reached with a modifying message, it will need to come from a source of authority they respect.

Herein lies the strength of using the biblical record of Jesus to critique at least Christian fundamentalism. Whether or not this can be done with other religious writings (for example, critiquing Islamic fundamentalism through the Qur'an) is a task I will leave for other writers, but I suspect that it would be difficult. For Christians, the teachings and example of Christ are not just one more portion of the Bible, equal among others. Christ's life and message form the centerpiece of the Bible to which every other aspect of scriptural teaching points toward or reflects on. This qualifies Jesus to stand as the authoritative judge of fundamentalists who randomly quote verses from the Bible to justify war, slavery, or sexism. But before we examine the message and mission of Jesus in detail, let's look at some more examples of the destructive nature of religious fundamentalism.

Terrorism. After the horrific events of September 11, 2001, news networks interviewed many *Western* Muslim scholars who reassured viewers that Islam is a religion of peace. That may be their conviction, but many of the world's Muslims (the ones with the bombs) would view those very scholars as apostates, liberal traitors to the faith as outlined in their own scriptures. Hence, the words of comfort offered by moderate Muslims mean little to the targets of Islamic fundamentalists. For me, moderates are not adequate spokespersons for their faith. Sam Harris comments, "Anyone who says that the doctrines of Islam have 'nothing to do with terrorism'—and our airways have been filled with apologists for Islam making this claim—is just playing a game with words."[1]

Moderate Muslims often point out that *jihad* is a word used in the Qur'an to describe inner struggle against sin and toward godliness. This is certainly true, but only half-true. Yes, *jihad* means "struggle" or "striving," and it can refer to inner spiritual striving to do the right thing. Nevertheless, as Muhammad demonstrated, the word also incorporates the idea of external struggle through religious warfare. According to the Institute of Islamic Information and Education in Chicago,

> Prophet Muhammad(S) undertook a number of armed campaigns to remove treacherous people from power and their lodgings. He had entered into pacts with several tribes, however, some of them proved themselves treacherous. Prophet Muhammad(S) launched armed campaigns against these tribes, defeated and exiled them from Medina and its surroundings. . . . Indeed, it is difficult to mobilize people to fight when they see no invaders in their territory; however, those who are charged with responsibility see dangers ahead of time and must provide leadership. The Messenger of Allah, Muhammad(S), had the responsibility to protect his people and the religion he established in Arabia. Whenever he received intelligence reports about enemies gathering near his borders he carried out pre-emptive strikes, broke their power and dispersed them. Allah ordered Muslims in the Qur'an:

"Fighting is prescribed upon you, and you dislike it.
But it may happen that you dislike a thing which is
good for you, and it may happen that you love a thing
which is bad for you. And Allah knows and you know
not." 2:216[2]

Although, on the one hand, the Qur'an teaches that Muslims
are supposed to use violence only as a form of defense (22:39-40),
Muhammad modeled the use of preemptive strikes as a form of allowable "defense" when feeling threatened. Do you see the problem here?
Muhammad opens up the possibility of all kinds of justifiable attacks
under the banner of preemptive strikes, all in the name of religious zeal.
We cannot escape the terrible truth that Muhammad modeled violence
as a supposedly righteous means to advance the earthly kingdom of
Islam. This means that we cannot consider those Muslims who use violence today to be completely outside the boundaries of authentic Muslim
religion. Violent Muslims are not a radical fringe element of Islam. Their
interpretation and application of the Qur'an grows out of the example
of Muhammad himself, even if taken to an extreme, and so is at least as
valid as that of the less violent moderates.[3] Our Muslim neighbors need
to listen again to the teachings of the one they call a prophet—Jesus.

But Islam is not the only form of religion to spawn violent fundamentalists. We have already looked at some of the horrors perpetrated
under the banner of Christianity, and we will not be able to avoid seeing
more. But what about other world religions?

First of all, take a moment to see if you can identify this scene taken
from the pages of religious history:

Mothers were skewered on swords as their children watched.
Young women were stripped and raped in broad daylight, then
doused . . . and set on fire. A pregnant woman's belly was slit
open, her fetus raised skyward on the tip of a sword and then
tossed onto one of the fires that blazed across the city.

When I speak on this topic in university settings, I often read the above paragraph and ask the audience to try to identify the event. The number one guess is always the Crusades—which should remind Christians of the reputation the church still holds in our world today. Stand in a secular setting and read a paragraph describing horrific violence and people respond, "How horrible. That must be describing Christians."

Is this a scene from the Crusades or some ancient tribal war? Today's world might seem like a kinder, gentler place if it were. The above passage describes a taste of the violence that erupted between Hindus and Muslims in India in the spring of 2002, as described in the *New York Times*.[4] Over one thousand people died in this monthlong series of riots. Religious differences were the primary motivating factor. Unfortunately, killing in the name of religion is not just a matter of ancient history, but is a significant aspect of the present-day world in which we live. In fact, in the time it will take you to read the rest of this chapter, someone somewhere on the planet will likely die because of religion.

Human Sacrifice. Fundamentalism is nothing new. The Aztecs and Mayans, like the ancient Ammonites mentioned in the Bible, used human sacrifice to appease their gods. Their grisly ceremonies could include live burnings, disembowelments, and sacred cannibalism—all in the service of religious worship. I wish we could say the gruesome scenes of human sacrifice in Mel Gibson's movie *Apocalypto* were exaggerated, but unfortunately they point back to a very dark reality. Anthropologists believe that the Aztecs sacrificed thousands of people, often children, to their gods every year.

Duty and Detachment. Ancient texts of most world religions contain the seed of violence in passages that become murderous in the hands of fundamentalists. The Hindu scriptures, the Bhagavad Gita, record the conversation between Lord Krishna and Arjuna, a warrior about to go into battle. When Arjuna realizes that many of his relatives are fighting in the opposing army, he questions Krishna on the morality of killing his family members for the sake of an earthly kingdom: "I do not see how any good can come from killing my own kinsmen in this battle, nor can I, my dear Krishna, desire any subsequent victory, kingdom, or happiness" (1:31).

Arjuna even catches a glimpse of what Jesus would later teach — that it is better to die for a cause than to kill for a cause: "Better for me if the sons of Dhrtarastra, weapons in hand, were to kill me unarmed and unresisting on the battlefield" (1:45).

Krishna responds to Arjuna by labeling his thoughts "impurities" (2:2) and calls him to "give up such petty weakness of heart" (2:3) and arise to kill his enemy. Krishna tells Arjuna not to worry about any one individual, but to do his "religious duty," the thing his caste has prepared him to do, because "you should know that there is no better engagement for you than fighting on religious principles; and so there is no need for hesitation" (2:31). Krishna goes on to offer the following teaching:

> "If, however, you do not perform your religious duty of fighting, then you will certainly incur sins for neglecting your duties and thus lose your reputation as a fighter." (2:33)

> "Do thou fight for the sake of fighting, without considering happiness or distress, loss or gain, victory or defeat — and by so doing you shall never incur sin." (2:38)

> "You have a right to perform your prescribed duty, but you are not entitled to the fruits of action. Never consider yourself the cause of the results of your activities, and never be attached to not doing your duty. Perform your duty equipoised, O Arjuna, abandoning all attachment to success or failure. Such equanimity is called yoga." (2:47-48)

Be detached and do your duty. Don't think, just act. Play your part in the system of things and live out what your position prescribes for you. How many horrors have been successfully perpetrated because too many men held the attitude that "It wasn't my choice—I was just doing my duty"?

Reincarnation and Sati. Both Hinduism and Buddhism teach that the lives we are living at present are not our first and, most likely, not our last. We are caught in an unwanted cycle of rebirth from which we should seek to be freed. Many westerners have, as westerners do, decided that they like this belief, but not without changing it, romanticizing it, westernizing it. We enjoy finding out that we may have been a duke or duchess, pirate or princess, an eagle, horse, or dolphin in a former life. But not many people who believe in reincarnation talk about the important lessons they learned from their life as a cockroach or toe fungus, rapist or serial killer. These people have made the doctrine of reincarnation more "moderate" according to their own cultural sensitivities, but I'm left asking—do they really think this arbitrary editing and cultural imposition helps any of us get closer to the truth of life?

Although finally outlawed in the 1800s, for countless years religious Hindus praised widows who chose to commit suicide when their husbands died. This traditional practice, called *sati*, involved throwing themselves on the funeral pyre to burn with their dead husbands. Such a woman could die with the good hope of her reward: coming back again—as a man.

Some defenders of religion have tried to argue that *sati* is more of a cultural practice than a religious one, but this is grasping at straws. Such cultural practices could never become so well embraced without the powerful motivation that only religious underpinnings can provide.

Reincarnation and Karma. Reincarnation is linked with the Hindu and Buddhist doctrine of *karma*—a belief that offers a sense of ultimate and immediate justice for people who have trouble with delayed gratification. Because karma teaches that whatever happens to people is brought upon themselves by their own deeds (whether in this life or a past life), it has particular appeal to people who want a simple and immediate explanation for the pain and suffering of our planet.

According to the Vedas (the sacred texts of Hinduism), if we sow goodness, we will reap goodness; if we sow evil, we will reap evil. Although similar to one strain of Christian teaching (see Galatians 6:7-9), it can have destructive consequences when partnered with the doctrine of reincarnation, because current suffering can be explained as the harvest for what was sown in a past life. Rather than motivating people to partner with God to bring justice and mercy to this unfair world, karma allows people to believe that everything *is* just and fair *now*. Those who suffer are suffering because they are *supposed* to suffer; they *deserve* to suffer. It is their karma.[5]

Philosophers have long pointed out the inherent danger of this belief system. Logically, to help prevent someone's suffering in this life is only to postpone the inevitable and to consign him to return again to suffer more in his next life. So, with absolute clarity of conscience, a practicing Hindu can logically ignore his or her suffering neighbors, knowing that their suffering is just and a necessary step to their finally attaining salvation.

It is not surprising that India's caste system evolved within this system of belief. Those born into prosperity have arrived into that caste justly and are under no compulsion to help those born into poverty, who likewise are justly born into their caste. Each life is working off its own karmic debt and should not be interfered with lest you merely delay that life's entrance into salvation. For thousands of years, this belief has led to immeasurable suffering. It is understandable why Gandhi rejected this aspect of his religion of origin.

One of the reasons Western people have been attracted to Hinduism and Buddhism is that karma replaces the Judeo-Christian concept of "sin," arguably a less-than-popular concept. But rightly understood, sin is a good-news idea. As we'll see in later chapters, Jesus taught that sin is forgivable—karma, by definition, is not. Sin can be done away with by God's mercy. Karma must be worked off by each individual with no exceptions. In a world controlled by karma, there is no mercy, only justice. Karma must be worked off, no matter how much suffering that takes, spread out over as many lives as necessary. I for one would like to think of my failings as sin rather than karma, an aspect of my life that is done away with through God's compassion rather than by the necessity of my living multiple lives of suffering in order to work it off. I'm glad Jesus clearly rejected the idea of karma (see Luke 13:1-5; John 9:1-3) while offering people God's complete forgiveness for all sin.

Karma and Violence. One might expect that the doctrine of *ahimsa*—nonviolence—would prevent Buddhists from making it into the Religious Violence Hall of Fame. Unfortunately, as Mark Juergensmeyer reports in his book *Terror in the Mind of God*, "The history and teachings of Buddhism are not spotless. The great military conquests of the Sinhalese kingdoms in Sri Lanka, for instance, have been conducted in the name of Buddhist tradition and often with the blessings of Buddhist monks."[6]

Juergensmeyer points out that Buddhists can interpret the doctrine of karma as a law that invites holy people to partner with it. For instance, if a ruler is perceived as an enemy of the good, it is right to fight against him or her, in the name of karma. In fact, murdering someone who is living a life of bad karma becomes an act of mercy from this point of view, helping their souls move to a higher plane before they acquire more bad karma.

Perhaps this was the thinking of the Buddhist monk who killed the prime minister of Sri Lanka in 1959. The members of Aum Shinrikyo, an offshoot of Japanese Buddhism, explained a similar motivation in 1995, when they released poisonous sarin gas in the Tokyo subway, killing a number of commuters and injuring nearly a thousand more.

Christian Fundamentalism. Because the holy texts of nearly all religions hold the seed of violence, fundamentalists of every stripe tend to become increasingly violent, in their attitudes if not in their actions.[7] William Temple, former Archbishop of Canterbury, insisted that if our concept of God is wrong, the more religious we get, the more dangerous we are to ourselves and others. But here is the strange thing about the Jesus faith (and I am not talking about the Christian religion in general, but those who follow the teachings and example of Jesus specifically): The more precisely someone commits to following his teachings as modeled by his example—in other words, the more of a *fundamentalist* someone becomes about the teachings of Jesus—the more loving, forgiving, and gracious that person should become.

The problem with many Christian fundamentalists is that they are not fundamentalist enough when it comes to *Jesus*. Please understand, whenever the Christian church has become violent or intolerant or just plain uncharitable, it is not because of a fundamentalist adherence to the teachings of Jesus, but precisely the opposite. It is because Christ's teachings have been patently ignored. Many Christian fundamentalists do not follow Christ, but have replaced his teachings with the prevailing conservative ethos of the day masquerading as religious dogma.

Other Christian fundamentalists replace following Jesus with following the Bible. These kinds of fundamentalists are often good-hearted people who are completely sincere, but sincerely wrong. I am thinking of those Christians who love God and are very dedicated to following the Bible, but fail to realize how the Bible is meant to be read. According to Jesus, the Bible is a developmental narrative that points toward and calls us to follow the gospel—the good news message of Jesus. The Old Testament and New Testament work together to form a kind of before-and-after picture (an idea developed further by the apostle Paul in the book of Galatians, and one that we will return to later). Jesus claimed that just following the Bible is not enough. He said that we must use the Bible to point us to him, and then follow his teaching and example. This was his complaint against the Pharisees, the main Bible-thumping fundamentalist group of his day. Today's Christian fundamentalists (or, more accurately, *Bible* fundamentalists) need to hear afresh these words of Jesus (to the Pharisees): "You search the Scriptures because you think they give you eternal life. But the Scriptures point to me! Yet you refuse to come to me to receive this life" (John 5:39-40, NLT; also see Luke 4:16-21; 24:25-27,44-47).

Let me submit a case study of Bible fundamentalism gone wild. In

1994, Rev. Paul J. Hill shot and killed Dr. John Britton on his way to
work at an abortion clinic, along with his volunteer escort, Jim Barrett.
Hill was motivated to kill because of his understanding of and dedication to the Bible. This becomes evident when reading the book he wrote
from death row explaining his biblical motivations, *Mix My Blood with
the Blood of the Unborn*.[8] Here we have a dedicated evangelical fundamentalist pastor—and there are others—who advocates killing in order
to protect unborn babies in the name of his Christian faith. To him and
others who share his views, it all makes sense from a *biblical* perspective.
After all, doesn't the Bible command God's people to "defend the rights
of the afflicted and needy" (Proverbs 31:9, NASB) and to "rescue those
being led away to death" (Proverbs 24:11)? And shouldn't we use force,
even deadly force, in order to protect those who cannot protect themselves? After all, isn't the Bible full of examples of God's people using
deadly force to do God's will?

Yes, people should partner with God to bring about justice and
compassion for the weak and outcasts, but Jesus shows the way to do
that—and the way *not* to do that. He teaches clearly that his followers must be willing, not to take lives, but to lay down their lives in the
service of the poor, the oppressed, the afflicted, weak, and needy. Our
example comes from Jesus himself: "This is how we know what love
is: Christ gave his life for us. We too, then, ought to give our lives for
others!" (1 John 3:16, TEV; also see John 10:11; 15:12-13).

Jesus commands his followers to imitate his example of self-
sacrificing love as the way to bring about positive change. Paul Hill was
not murderously violent because he followed Jesus' teaching and example, but because he *neglected* to follow Jesus. In an attempt to follow the
Bible, Christian fundamentalists like Hill fail to follow Jesus. Christ
was clear—the way to bring about meaningful change is to lay your life
down, not take another's.

Yes, if someone reads portions of the Bible without accepting the
way of Jesus as the focal point of it all, then they will find passages to
justify violence, but that is not reading the Bible like a Christ-follower.

"Christ," said the apostle Paul, "is the culmination of the law" (Romans 10:4) where *culmination* translates the Greek word *telos*, meaning end-goal. Everything in the Bible points toward Jesus, said Paul. Now follow Jesus—his teaching, his example. Allow his example to interpret the Bible for you.

During some of the most violent times of church history, Christians were obsessive about biblical accuracy and theological purity, but that was part of the problem. The Apostles' Creed, for example, skips from "born of a virgin" straight to "suffered under Pontius Pilate." Did no one think that Christians were missing something here? How about the entire life, teachings, and example of Jesus? Brian McLaren writes, "Contrast the flood of man-hours by the church debating esoteric theological/philosophical issues with the comparative trickle of attention paid to understanding and applying Jesus' kingdom ethics; the difference is staggering."[9]

Real Christ-followers are those who, having been on the receiving end of God's gracious love through Jesus, pour out this same embracing love to others in ways that mend broken relationships, heal inner wounds, and offer practical care for the helpless and hurting.

This is why we often say at my church, The Meeting House, that when it comes to Jesus—not the Bible in general, but Jesus in particular—we want to be *more* "fundamentalist" than the fundamentalists. We want to passionately live out the teachings of Jesus in our daily lives with no cultural compromise. We want the words of Hebrews 12:2 to describe our experience: "Let us keep our eyes fixed on Jesus, on whom our faith depends from beginning to end" (Hebrews 12:2, TEV).

For those of us who claim to be Christ-followers (what the word "Christian" means), then our goal is simple—we should follow Christ. We must focus on Jesus. He originates and guides true Christian faith. The example he leaves us is one of other-centered, self-sacrificing love. Oh, how I wish that were true of all those who call themselves "Christians," myself included!

As we will see in the next sections of this book, following Jesus will move us toward his countercultural way of limitless forgiveness, radical acceptance, nonviolent peacemaking, and sacrificial love. It will also move us away from dependence on religious systems as our pathway to God.

Q & Eн?

1. Why are the moderates within any one religious group not well equipped to bring about reform within that religion?

2. How can the doctrines of karma and reincarnation lead to increased human suffering?

3. If Christians believe (a) that a fetus is an unborn, innocent child and (b) that violence is an acceptable way for Christians to work for justice, then what is to prevent the pro-life movement from killing abortion doctors?

4. Describe a picture of what someone who radically follows the teaching of Jesus—a real *Jesus* fundamentalist—might look like today.

This is how we know what love is: Christ gave his life for us.
We too, then, ought to give our lives for others!

— 1 JOHN 3:16, TEV

———◆◆◆———

PART TWO

A
SCANDALOUS
LIFE

———◆◆◆———

*Two thousand years ago God started a revolt against the
religion He started. So don't ever put it past God to cause a
groundswell movement against churches and Christian institutions that bear His name. If He was willing to turn Judaism
upside down, don't think for a moment our institutions are safe
from a divine revolt. I am convinced that even now there are
multitudes of followers of Jesus Christ who are sick and tired
of the church playing games and playing down the call of God.
My travels only confirm that the murmurings of revolution are
everywhere. I am convinced that there is an uprising in the
works and that no one less than God is behind it.*
— ERWIN MCMANUS

CHAPTER SIX

Taking On the Establishment

It is no surprise, in view of his teachings and actions, that Jesus was crucified. What is surprising is that it did not happen sooner.
— BEN WITHERINGTON III

In the first part of this book I claimed that Jesus' offensive actions of turning water into wine were the tip of an irreligious iceberg. In this next section, we are going to dive beneath the surface to see just how deep the scandal goes. We will see how the actions as well as the teachings of Jesus reveal a clearly irreligious agenda that bypasses the salvation system of his day to connect us directly with God. Then, in the final section, we will explore some of the implications of the subversive spirituality of Jesus for our day.

To fully appreciate the scandalous nature of Jesus' life, we need to get a better understanding of the socioreligious context within which Jesus lived and taught. Sadly, many popular spiritual teachers and authors fail us at this point. In their rush to make the meaning of Jesus' teachings universal, authors forget (or intentionally ignore?) the particular context within which his words were spoken—the world of first-century Israel. Like any message, when we lift Jesus' teachings out of their context, we can make Jesus say almost anything we like, rather than what he intended.

I believe Jesus' life holds universal significance for us, but we will understand that significance if we see what he was saying first within his own cultural and historical framework. Once we understand what he meant in particular terms, within the religious debates of his day, then we will more easily see the universal lessons, the transferable principles that we can apply to all spiritual matters in every day. Therefore, I offer this word of caution: Beware of those spiritual teachers who talk about Christ in cosmic terms without rigorous commitment to helping us understand him in historical terms. The profound beauty of his message is lost if we miss either of these aspects of the Christ event. Yes, it is a story of God's cosmic love, but it is also the story of that love entering our history in a particular expression. We must hold both in our minds at the same time. It is not just a story about a loving God, or a story about a compassionate man. It is the profound message of the one being revealed in the other.

The outrageously encouraging message of Jesus is that the Creator of the universe, the God of love, entered human history and lived among us incognito. The One who is before and beyond all things—that is, the Grand Context for all of life—entered our human context. He lived a particular life, as a particular gender, in a particular place, at a particular time, as part of a particular people. I do not know why male and not female, why Jewish and not Irish, why first-century Israel and not twenty-first-century Canada. I have my theories, and perhaps you have yours. What I do know is that the particularity of Jesus—that is, being one thing and not being another thing—is the price of being human. Through Jesus, God paid that price and fully entered our human experience in a particular way.

Whether or not you approach Jesus as a source of *divine* revelation, I assume you're investing time in this book because we both agree that Jesus has something to say to us. If we want to understand what that message is, we need to acknowledge that it was not said in a vacuum. When we take the time to understand Jesus' first-century Jewish context, his words and actions come alive with meaning that we would have otherwise missed. This is the message of the next few chapters of this book. In a sense, Christ's challenge to the dominant religion of his historical context becomes for us a kind of case study, from which we can draw transferable principles into our own context. The examples are particular, but if we do the work to understand them, the spiritual wisdom we glean will be universal.

The religious people of first-century Israel considered various external characteristics of their faith to be central to their spiritual lives. These were badges of identity, boundary markers of unique status and calling. We could divide these external issues into five categories, all of which Jesus challenged in some way:[1]

- **Torah**: The Law of Moses was to be obeyed to the letter, including dietary laws and Sabbath regulations.
- **Tradition**: Keeping the "tradition of the elders" (or oral Torah) handed down from their ancestors was on par with obedience to Scripture (the written Torah).
- **Tribalism**: Ethnic, national, and cultural purity were bound together with religious identity.
- **Territory**: A theology of holy geography meant certain land, cities, and places were more sacred than others, and that war was a religious duty whenever this holy land was threatened.
- **Temple**: God's presence was believed to dwell in one holy location in a unique way where worshipers could offer sacrifices and receive forgiveness.

Notice that each of these identity-markers engenders exclusivity. Together they helped prop up a strong us-and-them mentality between Israel and the rest of the world.

Yes, God had granted Israel special status, but that status was not an end in itself—it was a call to a particular mission. In keeping with his heart for partnership, God had *entrusted* his message of love to Israel so they might carry his message to all the people of the world (see Genesis 12:3; 18:18; 22:18; 26:4; Isaiah 2:2-4; 42:6; 49:6; Micah 4:1-7;

Zechariah 8:20-23; Matthew 5:14-16; Romans 3:2). Instead, Israel was using the Word they had received from God as a religious and cultural blockade, keeping them separated from the world around them and preventing them from fulfilling their mission to bring the light of God's love to others.

Here is a silly scene that helps make my point. Picture a DJ at a large urban club. He is having a fantastic time, dancing behind his turntables with his headphones on, totally immersed in his music. But there is a problem—the DJ never thought to turn on the main speakers! Look out on the dance floor and watch the people standing there, waiting in silence (imagine the sound of crickets, just for the fun of it). This DJ might have awesome music, but he has missed the point of *why* he has the music.

Or think of this absurd scenario described by N. T. Wright. Picture a letter carrier who is proud of his big bag of mail. In fact, he is so proud of it that he wears it everywhere he goes like a badge of honor for all to see. "Look how popular I am," he tells his friends. "I have so much mail." He has forgotten that his purpose is to *deliver* what he has been *entrusted* with.[2]

Jesus blew apart the facade of his religious contemporaries. He reprimanded them for having forgotten their purpose. He exposed the ways they had replaced their mission to bring light to the world with high religious walls that kept all "sinners" away.

In the following chapters we'll see how, one by one, Jesus contested the popular understanding of each of Israel's group identity-markers. As we go, take note of how scandalous his life and teachings were from a religious point of view. It was all part of his plan to dismantle religious barricades then and now, and to make a way into his more radically inclusive kingdom.

At this point, it is worth noting something important. Read the New Testament and you will see that Jesus is very hard on the religious leaders of his day. He often condemns them for their hypocrisy, blindness, and hard-heartedness. Because they are leaders of the Jewish religion, some people have concluded that Jesus or the New Testament authors are somehow anti-Jewish or anti-Judaism. Nothing could be further from the truth.

The Jesus of the Bible is no more anti-Jewish than was Isaiah, Jeremiah, Amos, or any other Hebrew prophet who criticized Israel for missing the mark in their day. Please understand, Jesus' challenge to his contemporary Jewish leaders represents a critique *from within*. It is an "in-house" debate, motivated by love. His harsh words against Jerusalem, the temple, or the religious leaders are not motivated by any anti-Jewish sentiments, but exactly the opposite. *Jesus critiques the Jewish religious leaders because they are religious, not because they are Jewish.* And if we grab hold of that, we can see how his rebukes are transferable for all religions at all times.

Q & Eh?

1. Part 2 began with a quote by Erwin McManus. What do you think about the brewing "revolution" he is describing?

2. Why is it important to study the teachings of Jesus within their first-century Jewish context? If we do that, how can we draw out the universal truths for our lives today?

3. Let's do some brain stretches:

   - Of the five group "identity-markers" listed in this chapter, can you think of examples of how Jesus challenged each one?
   - Can you think of contemporary examples of how religious people today argue over any of these same issues?

4. What are your thoughts about the following quotes by William C. Placher and Beverly Roberts Gaventa:

- If we acknowledge that the Pharisees were the respectable, pious people of the time, then we have to admit that Jesus had little patience with respectable, pious people.[3]
- The Pharisees were good, faithful, religious people of their day. And it is good, faithful, religious people of every era who find themselves in conflict with Jesus.[4]

5. During long seasons of church history, Christians interpreted Jesus' condemnation of many Jewish religious practices as God's condemnation of Jews. How can we avoid making this destructive mistake today?

What advantage, then, is there in being a Jew, or what value
is there in circumcision? Much in every way! First of all,
the Jews have been entrusted with the very words of God.

— ROMANS 3:1-2

CHAPTER SEVEN

Breaking the Rules

Overriding Torah

Maybe the poets are right. Maybe love is the only answer.
— WOODY ALLEN

In the middle of his Sermon on the Mount when Jesus says, "Treat others as you want them to treat you. This is what the Law and the Prophets are all about" (Matthew 7:12, CEV), he is touching on universal wisdom. Another ancient Jewish teacher, Rabbi Hillel, said, "What is hateful to yourself, do not do to your fellow man. That is the whole of the Torah" (Talmud, Shabbat 31a). Predating both Jesus and Hillel, the Buddha taught, "Consider others as yourself." Confucius expressed this principle in a similar way to Hillel when he also taught, "What one does not wish for oneself, one ought not to do to anyone else."

Although Jesus was not the first to allude to this idea, he is the first to express it as an unmistakably positive call to action. Rather than emphasize what *not* to do, as Hillel and Confucius do (Buddha is ambiguous), Jesus clearly challenges his followers to take the initiative to love, to look for ways to take care of others' needs, just as we do for ourselves: Do unto others as you would have them do unto you (also see Matthew 22:39).

This emphasis on other-focused action has been called the Golden Rule (especially as it is expressed in Matthew 7:12), and it sits as the epicenter of Jesus' teaching on faith, religion, and ethics. It is, however, more than a "rule." Rules often make sense only within one context. Change the context and the rules' value disappears. In Canada, for instance, driving on the right side of the road is a rule. But this rule would be counterproductive in England. Hence, Jesus offers us a transcendent *principle*, a guiding *orientation*, a directing *ethic* that is transferable to all situations.

The Jesus of the Bible lives by a simple philosophy: If love guides our hearts, rules become redundant. Love, embraced as a guiding orientation of other-centeredness, will always lead us to do the right thing.

To make his point about love replacing law, Jesus sets out to deconstruct the rule-based system of the religion of his day. Before he can build for people a new understanding of a love-led life, he first has to tear down the old law-based edifice. So Jesus lives in such a way as to offend those who put their faith in religious rules rather than in the way of love.

Look at the following examples:

- Even though the Old Testament contains many dietary rules about what constitutes kosher food and what does not (see Leviticus 11), Jesus declares all foods clean (Mark 7:18-19).
- Even though Moses had commanded very clear procedures concerning divorce and remarriage (see Deuteronomy 24:1-4), Jesus teaches that God meant these rules to be a temporary compromise because of the hardness of the human heart and that he had come to offer a better way (see Matthew 5:31-32; 19:8-9).
- Even though carrying personal belongings around on the Sabbath was forbidden by the Old Testament Scriptures (see Exodus 20:9-11; Jeremiah 17:21-22,27), when Jesus heals a paralyzed man on the Sabbath, he specifically commands him

to "pick up your mat, and walk" (John 5:8-9, TEV). To add insult to injury, Jesus later refers to his healing as "working" (John 5:16-17) on the Sabbath, apparently for no other reason than to shock the interrogating religious leaders into deeper thought.

- And even though the Old Testament contains many rules about avoiding people with skin diseases (see Leviticus 13–14), Jesus heals lepers—with a touch (Matthew 8:3).

Jesus' call into a rule-free, principle-based spirituality is very difficult for religious people to fathom. Certainly, rule-less spirituality is only a constructive way to live *if* love is the guiding dynamic, the foundational principle of our lives. This is essential to Jesus' message. Jesus never made rule-breaking a worthy goal in and of itself. His point was that rule-keeping should be a natural expression of something deeper, rather than a goal unto itself (see Matthew 23:23). Simply remove rules and you are left with anarchy (see 1 John 3:4). Transcend rules with love, and you are beginning to live like Jesus.

For the religious leaders, Jesus' rule-breaking lifestyle appeared to expose his obvious disregard for Torah. For Jesus, his lifestyle was a more accurate way of living out the principles contained within the precepts of Torah. Although Jesus was repeatedly accused of abandoning Scripture, he defended his lifestyle by claiming to fulfill the true meaning of Scripture better than the religious leaders (see Matthew 5:17-20; 12:1-8).

In his famous Sermon on the Mount, Jesus explains his own relationship with Scripture:

Do not think that I have come to abolish the Law or the Prophets; I have not come to abolish them but to fulfill them. Truly I tell you, until heaven and earth disappear, not the smallest letter, not the least stroke of a pen, will by any means disappear from the Law until everything is accomplished. Anyone who sets aside one of the least of these commands and teaches others accordingly will be called least in the kingdom of heaven, but whoever practices and teaches these commands will be called great in the kingdom of heaven. For I tell you that unless your righteousness surpasses that of the Pharisees and the teachers of the law, you will certainly not enter the kingdom of heaven. (Matthew 5:17-20)

"Do not think that I have come to abolish the Law," Jesus says. Why would anyone think that? Why would Jesus need to assure his audience of his fidelity to the rules of Torah? What about Jesus' life and teaching left people wondering if he was calling them to abandon God's law? He gives us a clue in his follow-up comment. He hasn't come to abolish the Old Testament Scriptures, but he has come to *fulfill* them, to absorb them into his own life and teach us a better way of living out the very principles they contain. The religious leaders known as Pharisees were meticulous at obeying the letter of the law, but that is not the way, says Jesus. In fact, as meticulous as they were, Jesus says that our righteousness must *surpass* the righteousness of the Pharisees.

If a family of Pharisees moved into your neighborhood today, you would probably consider yourself quite fortunate. They would be upstanding citizens, actively involved in community life. They would be enthusiastic contributors to your Neighborhood Watch program. You would notice that they never turn away a representative from a local charity who comes to their door for a donation and that their lifestyle, like their home, is always neat and tidy. Oh sure, you may have to put up with the occasional knock on your door by smiling, Bible-toting missionaries from that family wanting to share their love of the Lord with you, but that wouldn't be so bad. At least you wouldn't have to put up with any loud parties, and you would know that their children could be counted on to be a positive influence on yours.

The truth is, they would seem like such wonderful people that—if anything—you would feel like *you* needed to do better with *your* life.

You may even be a little intimidated because they would seem to have it all so "together." Occasionally you might wonder, "Don't they have *any* vices?"

That's why you would be startled if Jesus showed up and told you the same thing he told the people of his day: "For I tell you that unless your righteousness surpasses that of the Pharisees and the teachers of the law, you will certainly not enter the kingdom of heaven" (Matthew 5:20).

What? We have to be better people than that hyper-devout Pharisee family to enter God's kingdom? I can hear your thoughts from here: "But I know that family—they're so 'perfect' they make me sick! How in the world could *I* ever please God if *they* don't?"

Perhaps you're getting a small taste of what the Jews of Jesus' day would have gone through upon hearing these words in the middle of his Sermon on the Mount. They would have been shocked—and perhaps overwhelmed—because the Pharisees were cultural icons of righteousness. The apostle Paul, himself a former Pharisee, describes them as the "strictest sect of our religion" (Acts 26:5, NASB). The Pharisees were passionate rule-keepers. They were the Bible-fundamentalists of their day. If they had a motto it would have been, "The Bible says it. That settles it. I believe it. Let's do it." But according to Jesus, that is not enough. Following the letter of the law is dangerous, as witch-burning, war-fighting, pagan-killing Christianity attests. Jesus calls us to use Scripture to get to know God's heart, to see God's love expressed through Jesus, and to follow *him*. To the Pharisees in his day and our day, Jesus says: "You carefully study the Scriptures because you think *they* give you eternal life. They do in fact tell about me, but you refuse to come to me to have that life" (John 5:39-40, NCV, emphasis added).

I once tried to explain this concept to my girls while reading a bedtime Bible story. They were quite puzzled by the fact that Jesus, the "hero" of the story, was the one breaking all the rules and getting into so much trouble. I had to find a way to explain to them that love must always overcome law. The lights finally went on when I gave them this example:

"Suppose you got a wonderful new dress for an upcoming wedding," I started. "Because you liked it so much, you asked if you could wear it to school the next day, rather than waiting until the weekend wedding. What if I told you that you could wear your new dress to school if you wanted to, but only if you obeyed this simple rule: You must not get the dress dirty. This would mean that you would have to sit out from playing any sports at recess and would have to be extra careful in class. Would that be a fair rule?" They agreed it would be. "Then what if you set out for school the next day with your new dress on, only to come across a friend who had fallen off her bike and landed in a muddy ditch. What if your friend was hurt and needed help. What should you do?"

It didn't take my daughters long to express the right answer, the *loving* answer. "We should help her," they said. I told them I was happy to hear that answer and completely agreed, but reminded them that, in all likelihood, they would get their new dress completely dirty. "That doesn't matter as much," they said. "Helping our friend is more important."

"Are you *sure*?" I pushed. "What about the *rule*? What do you think my reaction would be if you came home all dirty from head to toe?"

"You would be proud of us for doing the right thing," they answered. And they were right. They got it. It was one of those moments parents live for.

I explained to them that in Jesus' day many religious leaders focused on keeping their dresses clean. (When my daughters objected that they probably didn't wear dresses I assured them that this was quite beside the point.) The religious leaders of Jesus' day focused on obeying the rules and often forgot to put love first. Jesus came to recalibrate the whole system.

Rather than give us new rules, Jesus took the principles embedded within the rules and wrapped them in a human life. So the entire life of Jesus, his teachings and his example, becomes "God's Word" to us. This is good news, because it is easier, or at least clearer, to follow an example of a person than to try to translate into living action a collection of commandments that have no context.

Jesus called his followers to live by a higher standard, the way of love instead of the way of law (see Matthew 7:12). And to drive home his point, he had to break the rules over and over again.

Q & Eʜ?

1. How is the truth encased in the Golden Rule (a) universal spiritual teaching? (b) unique to Jesus?

2. How do you think religious leaders would have reacted to Jesus going out of his way to break the rules of their Holy Scriptures?

3. According to Jesus, what role should the Bible play in the lives of his followers?

4. If Jesus liberates his followers from the necessity of rule-keeping, what is to prevent them from living lives of total anarchy?

For Christ has brought the Law to an end,
so that everyone who believes is put right with God.

— ROMANS 10:4, TEV

CHAPTER EIGHT

A Fence Around the Law

Trouncing Tradition

Jesus will not be domesticated.
— JOHN PIPER

The religious leaders of Jesus' day thought they had a terrific way of helping people apply the commands of Scripture to every aspect of their day-to-day lives. They verbally passed on from generation to generation extra traditions to accompany and expand upon the written Torah, the Law given through Moses. These extra rules were called the "tradition of the elders," or oral Torah. They were considered "a fence around the law." Based on the better-safe-than-sorry principle, these fences of tradition were designed to ensure people stayed conservative, conventional, conformist, and supposedly far from sin. In order to break a law and thereby fall into sin, a person would first have to intentionally "hop the fence" of tradition.

If Jesus was willing to break the rules of the Bible to make his point, he was even more merciless on inherited religious tradition. *Fences are fine for cattle, but sheep need a Shepherd.*

Jesus and his disciples opted out of what were very important religious traditions in first-century Judaism. For instance, remember the holy hand-washing ritual described in chapter 1? As you might expect, Jesus and his disciples did not participate in this sacred tradition. When the religious leaders challenged them on the issue, wanting everyone to conform to the norm, Jesus defended his position by going on the offensive.

> The Pharisees and some of the teachers of the law who had come from Jerusalem gathered around Jesus and saw some of his disciples eating food with hands that were defiled, that is, unwashed. (The Pharisees and all the Jews do not eat unless they give their hands a ceremonial washing, holding to the tradition of the elders. When they come from the marketplace they do not eat unless they wash. And they observe many other traditions, such as the washing of cups, pitchers and kettles.)
>
> So the Pharisees and teachers of the law asked Jesus, "Why don't your disciples live according to the tradition of the elders instead of eating their food with defiled hands?"
>
> He replied, "Isaiah was right when he prophesied about you hypocrites; as it is written:
>
>> "'These people honor me with their lips,
>>   but their hearts are far from me.
>> They worship me in vain;
>>   their teachings are merely human rules.'
>
> You have let go of the commands of God and are holding on to human traditions."
>
> And he continued, "You have a fine way of setting aside the commands of God in order to observe your own traditions!" (Mark 7:1-9)

In a different translation Jesus chides the Pharisees, "You are experts at setting aside the commandment of God in order to keep your tradition" (Mark 7:9, NASB). Then later, "By your own rules, which you teach people, you are rejecting what God said" (Mark 7:13, NCV).[1] These would be shocking words to people who believed their traditions reflected God's will as much as Scripture.[2]

Jesus makes it clear that tradition must take a backseat to the Scripture it claims to be based on. Furthermore, Jesus believes that even the Scriptures themselves must submit to his own authoritative interpretation. Jesus considers his own authority, not religious tradition, the first and last word on how to interpret and apply the Bible.

This does not mean that traditions can never be helpful spiritual tools. The New Testament speaks positively of traditions on more than one occasion (see 1 Corinthians 11:2; 2 Thessalonians 2:15; 3:6). At the same time, the New Testament also contains strong cautions about religious tradition (see Matthew 15:1-20; Colossians 2:8). So why would Jesus and his earliest followers give religious traditions, at best, mixed reviews? The answer, I think, may be found in the origin and evolution of religious traditions.

We can illustrate how traditions evolve by making up a hypothetical biblical law. Let's pretend God clearly communicated through Scripture that, for reasons known only to him, it is wrong for his people to sit in red chairs. (Remember, this is a symbolic exercise — I have it on good authority that God actually likes red chairs.)

So God's Torah says, "Thou shalt not sit in red chairs." The role of spiritual leaders would be to communicate this teaching to each generation, and perhaps to suggest ways that this rule could best be maintained in their particular day and age. So the next generation of religious leaders makes a suggestion: "God's people should never be within ten feet of a red chair." This "fence" is designed as a helpful tool to aid people in their desire to obey God's law, but now an insidious process has begun.

The next generation inherits that new *suggestion* as a *rule* and tacks on their own "helpful" addition: "It is wrong for God's people to even look at red chairs." There, that should help people deal with the problem of temptation. Further generations add: "God's people must never be in the same room as a red chair" then "in the same house as a red chair" and so on. Eventually, most of the religious leaders' time is taken up debating whether or not it is spiritually lawful to shop at IKEA! A whole lineage of rules and regulations that God never intended thus evolves around this one topic. Sin-avoidance has been systematized, righteousness has been mechanized, and little room is left for deviation and diversity.

Like a holy snowball, the religious tradition in Jesus' day had grown heavier than people could bear. The rules had begun to rule and that was Christ's primary complaint against the tradition of the elders. Rather than help people move closer to God, as the religious leaders no doubt originally intended, their religious traditions had become a collection of "heavy burdens" (Jesus' words) that were a stumbling block to simple faith (see Matthew 23:4). Jesus had little tolerance for those teachings that made faith a complicated and burdensome matter.

And so even well-meaning traditions can sometimes discourage thoughtful faith. Although the first generation may have put great thought into the meaning of a new tradition, this doesn't guarantee that future generations will infuse the tradition with the same thoughtfulness. In fact, religious people often use traditions to do their thinking for them. In the end, traditions that claim to be "Bible-based" can subtly supplant Scripture in the lives of people who claim to follow the Bible. So while tradition is a mechanism we use to pass on truth to future generations, often only the mechanism gets passed on. To counter this, each new generation of believers must rediscover their roots and go back to the source teachings for themselves.

Reliance on religious traditions can create another danger—a false sense of security. Few people feel as spiritually safe as religious traditionalists do. After all, they have meticulously woven a pattern of serving the Almighty into their lives. How could he ever be displeased with them? They serve God by *habit* rather than by discerning choice. This tends to create blind spots for religious people and can even affect how they read their own sacred texts. They filter their understanding of Scripture through their traditions and routines and thereby usually come to conclusions that reaffirm their own traditions. More than once Jesus calls the religious leaders "blind guides" (see Matthew 15:14; 23:16,24). These blind spots make it easy for hypocrisy to take root, which was Jesus' main grievance against religious leaders (see Matthew 23:28; Luke 12:1, etc.).

I remember when I first noticed the power of tradition-induced blindness for myself. I admit up front that it seems like a trivial example, but it does clearly illustrate the acute spiritual myopia religious traditions can cause. I was at that age when, although I didn't mind going to church, I did mind having to get dressed up to go. For some people, putting on their nice clothes to attend religious services might be a way of symbolically honoring God and others, but for me it was just one big distraction. Sitting in the church pew, I had trouble focusing on anything other than how restricted I felt, contained within my itchy suit with the knot of my tie lingering just below my Adam's apple, as if to threaten strangulation at the slightest misbehavior. I wondered why God preferred this mild torture to jeans and a T-shirt. When I asked the adults, they explained that if the Queen came for a visit I would surely get dressed up to meet her. Therefore, shouldn't we get dressed up to meet the King of the universe? That reasoning seemed logical, so I assumed it must be true, even though in Sunday school I was taught Bible verses that said things like, "the LORD does not see as mortals see; they look on the outward appearance, but the LORD looks on the heart" (1 Samuel 16:7, NRSV).

As I grew older, my itchy suit and strangley tie motivated me to see for myself what the Bible says about how we should dress when worshipping God. I confess I was only studying the Bible on this topic because I was looking for loopholes, but I found more than that.

Jesus and the earliest leaders in his movement taught that Christ-followers should focus their attention on how they are dressed *on the inside*. Christ-followers are told to clothe themselves with Jesus (see Romans 13:14; Galatians 3:27), with their renewed selves (see Ephesians 4:24), with the spiritual armor of God (see Ephesians 6:11,14-17), with "compassion, kindness, humility, gentleness and patience" (Colossians 3:12-14; also see 1 Peter 5:5), and with perseverance and righteous acts (see Revelation 3:4-5; 19:7-8)—an emphasis in keeping with Old Testament teaching as well (see Psalm 132:16; Isaiah 61:10; Zechariah 3:3-5). In fact—and catch this—I discovered that the only Bible passages that address the issue of external appearance are those that, for various reasons, counsel Christians to intentionally dress *down* (see 1 Timothy 2:9-10; James 2:1-13; 1 Peter 3:3). I thought to myself, "And the truth will set you free!" (John 8:32).

Somewhere along the way, the institutional church developed a tradition of dressing *up* for Sunday services, and many religious Christians follow this tradition of the elders today, giving it the same weight as the Pharisees gave their traditions. Of course, since external appearance is not very important to God, people who want to get dressed up for church as a meaningful symbol of respect are welcome to do so. But biblically speaking, that is an allowance of grace, not a mandate for holiness. (We have many people who wear suits and ties or nice dresses at our church. We call them "visitors.")

Fascinatingly, many "Bible-based" Christians would tend to be judgmental of those who come to their church dressed down—as the Bible seems to support! This blinding power of tradition can, as this example demonstrates, cause people who are trying to follow the Bible to believe almost the exact *opposite* of what the Bible teaches. Even those who boast in their biblical underpinnings miss its plain teaching when tradition holds sway. Sadly, we could go on to many more examples of spiritual blindness caused by religious tradition, but I think you get the point.[3]

To the religious conservatives of his day, Jesus said, "Stop judging by external standards, and judge by true standards" (John 7:24, TEV). It seems to me that Jesus' rebukes against religion apply at least as much to present-day Christianity as they did to ancient Judaism.[4]

Jesus went out of his way to discount, disrespect, and dismantle blind adherence to inherited rituals, and he called his followers to flatten the fences of their tradition. The early church got the message and refused to pass on the oral Torah to future generations. When Mark wrote his gospel just a few decades after Jesus and mentioned the tradition of ritual washings, he had to explain what it was all about for his Christian readers (see Mark 7:3-4). So it seems as though at least the first few generations of Christ-followers didn't get bogged down with the religious traditions of their spiritual ancestors, but followed Christ's inside-out principles of purity (see Luke 11:41).

The great freedom and frustration of Christ-following is that the forms of this faith are open to diversity. You have to deal with that if you want to follow the way of Jesus. We cannot rely on inherited traditions to do the thinking for us, or else we may slowly devolve into something quite unlike what Jesus intended. This is, by the way, why I strongly believe in sticking closely to what the Bible teaches—not to be an oppressive legalist, but to *avoid* oppressive legalism. Remember that in Christian circles, legalism is usually the result of human tradition being added to the Bible and passed off as scriptural teaching. I find the original teachings of Jesus completely *freeing*! Why would anyone want to deviate from that?

Q & Eн?

1. As this chapter points out, the New Testament sometimes speaks positively about tradition. What do you think are some positive uses of tradition?

2. What are some ways that tradition can work against a person's spiritual growth? Can you give some examples?

3. Recall Jesus' first miracle as discussed in chapter 1. Jesus made a bold symbolic statement at the wedding in Cana when he desecrated the holy water jars with party wine, thereby prioritizing celebration over tradition. If Jesus came today, what sacred "tradition of the elders" do you think he would need to challenge in order to make his point?

4. Read over Mark 7:1-9 again. Jesus doesn't seem to be against all tradition, period. According to this text, what seems to be the secret for using traditions in a positive, healthy way?

See to it that no one takes you captive through hollow and deceptive philosophy, which depends on human tradition and the basic principles of this world rather than on Christ.

— COLOSSIANS 2:8, NIV

CHAPTER NINE

Family Values

Undoing Tribalism

One love, one heart.
Let's get together and feel all right.

— BOB MARLEY

Jesus' message of God's love was radically inclusive in a world where religions were anything but.

Ancient religions were tribal, defined by ethnic and political boundaries. Different people groups, nationalities, and city-states all worshipped their own god or gods. These deities would, not surprisingly, support the cultural and political agendas of the particular groups to which they belonged. Admittedly, this is not so different from the religious landscape of our day. Western Christians, for instance, have a longstanding tendency to confuse cross and flag, faith and nationalism, religion and politics.

It was into this world of competing deities that Jesus came with a strong rebuke. Although the focus of his message was on one particular ethnic religion that had lost touch with its global mission, the principles of his rebuke are universally transferable.

God has always had a plan to bless all people, Jew and Gentile, even though Jews were called by God for a specific task (see Genesis 17:18-29). God wanted to bless the world by working in partnership with a people. By calling Israel his "firstborn" son (see Exodus 4:22-23; Hosea 11:1), God indicated his intention to have more children. Israel was simply his first.

The ancient prophets called Israel to share what light they had with the entire world (see Genesis 12:3; 18:18; 22:18; 26:4; Isaiah 2:2-4; 42:6; 49:6; Micah 4:1-7; Zechariah 8:20-23; Romans 3:2). When Jesus came, he accused Israel of working against God's plan by keeping that light for themselves (see Matthew 5:14-16). Even though Jesus claimed he was sent first to help the Jews get back on course (see Matthew 10:5-6; 15:24), his message and mission intentionally extended God's offer of loving relationship beyond the ethnic boundaries of Jewish religion (see Romans 1:16). Through Jesus, Gentiles (non-Jews) were invited to become equal citizens in God's kingdom alongside Jewish brothers and sisters (see John 3:16; Luke 24:45-47; Romans 2:17-29; 4:9-18; 9:6; 10:11-13; Galatians 6:16; Ephesians 2:11-22; 1 Peter 2:9-10). As "king of the Jews," Jesus invites his own people to give up their claims of exclusivity and to join him in ushering in the universal sisterhood and brotherhood that faith can bring.

First-century Israel labored under Roman oppression and frequent attacks by neighboring Samaritans. Racial and religious tensions mixed together in what became a volatile cocktail. Religious discussions would quickly degenerate into debates over which race held land claims to Jerusalem (sound familiar?) and which ethnic group was truly God's chosen people. In response to one of these religious debates, Jesus told a scandalous story about a shocking hero. It began, like many conversations Jesus had, with a question:

One day an expert in religious law stood up to test Jesus by asking him this question: "Teacher, what must I do to receive eternal life?"

Jesus replied, "What does the law of Moses say? How do you read it?"

The man answered, "'You must love the LORD your God with all your heart, all your soul, all your strength, and all your mind.' And, 'Love your neighbor as yourself.'"

"Right!" Jesus told him. "Do this and you will live!"

The man wanted to justify his actions, so he asked Jesus, "And who is my neighbor?" (Luke 10:25-29, NLT)

Who is my neighbor? This is the question that draws out of Jesus what has become one of his most famous parables—sometimes called the parable of the Good Samaritan. Before we walk through that story, we need to understand the dialogue that leads up to it.

Jesus is being tested by a religious leader. The leader is aware that this rabbi from Nazareth takes a different approach to interpreting Torah, sometimes seeming to throw the holy Law aside altogether. As a representative of the religious establishment, it is his duty to do his best to expose Jesus for what he is—whatever that might be.

In the Hebrew Scriptures, God commands his people not only to love him, but also to "love your neighbor as yourself" (Leviticus 19:18). The context of this Old Covenant commandment suggests that "neighbor" applies only to other Israelites, and this is certainly how most Jews would have interpreted it in the days of Jesus.[1] So by asking Jesus the follow-up question of "Who is my neighbor?" the religious leader is challenging Jesus on something absolutely fundamental. He is asking Jesus to give his definition of the boundary-markers of God's kingdom: who is "in" and who is "out." Of course, his assumption is that, as a religious Jew, he is already "in," so by asking who his neighbor is, he is asking who is also "in" with him.

This is a deeply theological question for the religious leaders of Jesus' day. But it is also a very emotional issue at the same time. The *goyim* (that is, Gentiles, or non-Jews) that were known to first-century Jews were certainly not "neighbors" to them in any relational sense of the word.

The Romans were oppressors, pure and simple. And then there were those violent, unorthodox, hateful half-breeds, the Samaritans.[2] All this seemed clear enough to any self-respecting Jew in first-century Israel, but with Jesus' radical teaching on enemy-love, they must have wondered how he would interpret this Torah concept. And so, knowing that his definition of "neighbor" is a key component (perhaps *the* key component!) to understanding the teaching of this unconventional rabbi, the religious leader presses Jesus to define who he thinks his "neighbor" is.

Jesus knows that if we define "neighbor" only as those who are similar to us—people who are part of our own religious and/or ethnic community—then we will never stretch ourselves to love beyond those whom it is natural to love. Jesus instead calls us to a love that is supernatural. And so Jesus takes the world of his Jewish audience and turns it upside down and inside out. He not only stretches their definition of "neighbor" to include outcasts, but he makes an outcast the hero of the story!

> Jesus replied with a story: "A Jewish man was traveling on a trip from Jerusalem to Jericho, and he was attacked by bandits. They stripped him of his clothes, beat him up, and left him half dead beside the road.
>
> "By chance a priest came along. But when he saw the man lying there, he crossed to the other side of the road and passed him by. A Temple assistant walked over and looked at him lying there, but he also passed by on the other side." (Luke 10:30-32, NLT)

Stop right there. Before getting to the Samaritan bit, Jesus is already insulting the establishment by the role he assigns to the religious leaders in this story. He portrays their religious affiliation as a barrier rather than a motivator to becoming involved in the life of a hurting person.

But why would religious leaders behave in a way that is so disconnected from the obvious need before their eyes? Is this at all realistic? Unfortunately, what we know about religion at the time tells us it is. Jesus gives us a clue as to their motivation by pointing out that they did not just pass by, but they made sure they crossed over to the other side of the road while passing by. Religious leaders in first-century Israel believed people could be ritually contaminated by contact with a dead person—a contamination that would last for a full week, and could only be undone by ritual bathing (see Numbers 19:11-22). Priests especially were to avoid all contact with a corpse, except for family members (see Leviticus 21:1-11). Some believed that they would become ritually defiled if even their shadow touched a dead person.

So if these religious leaders were on their way to serve at the temple (which seems to be the case Jesus is making), this explains why they not only kept going, but made a point of staying on the other side of the road.[3] From a distance they would not have been able to tell if this naked, bleeding, and unconscious man at the side of the road was dead or not. And they were not willing to go close enough to find out lest he be dead and they be defiled. If they became ritually impure during this journey, they would become disqualified for temple service while on their way to serve there.[4] They may have rationalized that this was a case of the needs of the many having to be put ahead of the needs of the few. But Jesus sees it as putting religion ahead of relationship.

Tied up with the religion of first-century Israel was the powerful issue of race. From a distance, clothes were a visual cue for discerning who was a fellow Jew and who was a Samaritan, a Roman, or anything else. Since the victim's clothes were stolen, this man would have lost key distinguishing marks of which ethnic, political, religious group he belonged to. He was simply a human being in need. But human need was not enough information for our religious players in the story, illustrating that when religion and race mix, the resulting cocktail of exclusivity makes human value secondary.[5]

Jesus' audience no doubt picked up on the irreligious rhythm of his story as they watched the religious leaders pass by, too caught up in their religious duties to show practical love to a person in need. Still, nothing could have prepared them for the plot twist that followed. The story would have been challenging enough to his audience if the final traveler was a common Israelite who in the end was more helpful to his brother than a religious leader. This is probably what they would expect at this point.[6] It would be a parable against religious hypocrisy, sure, but at least it wouldn't be as insulting and offensive as it was about to become.

> "Then a despised Samaritan came along, and when he saw the man, he felt compassion for him. Going over to him, the Samaritan soothed his wounds with olive oil and wine and bandaged them. Then he put the man on his own donkey and took him to an inn, where he took care of him. The next day he handed the innkeeper two silver coins, telling him, 'Take care of this man. If his bill runs higher than this I'll pay you the next time I'm here.'" (Luke 10:33-35, NLT)

When a Samaritan shows up in the role of hero, all bets are off and all expectations are shattered. The Samaritans were not only considered to be outside of God's covenant people (and therefore, no "neighbor" to a Jew), they were ancient enemies. Donald B. Kraybill explains: "Bitter tension divided Jews and Samaritans. Samaria was sandwiched between Judea and Galilee. The Samaritans emerged about 400 BC from mixed marriages between Jews and Gentiles. The Jews regarded them as half-breed bastards."[7]

Not only was the ethnicity of Samaritans an insult to the purebred Jewish nation, but they created their own rival religious practices that made a mockery of Jewish belief. They had established their own temple and claimed that it was the true one, denouncing the Jewish temple in Jerusalem. In response, the Jews had destroyed the Samaritan temple. Then, when Jesus was about twelve years old, some Samaritans sneaked into the Jerusalem temple at night during Passover and scattered human bones over the temple sanctuary floor in order to desecrate it.[8] The Jews retaliated with more violence, and on and on the warfare went between them. Earlier in his public career, when the Jewish religious leaders wanted to insult Jesus, they called him "demon possessed." But when even that wasn't insulting enough, they also called him a "Samaritan" (John 8:48).

So as Alan Culpepper points out,

> By depicting a Samaritan as the hero of the story, therefore, Jesus demolished all boundary expectations. Social position—race, religion, or region—count for nothing. . . . The alteration of the expected sequence by naming the third character as a Samaritan not only challenges the hearer to examine the stereotypes regarding Samaritans, but it also invalidates all stereotypes. Community can no longer be defined or limited by such terms. . . . Jesus' parable, therefore, shatters the stereotypes of social boundaries and class division and renders void any system of religious quid pro quo. Neighbors do not recognize social class. . . . Eternal life—the life of the age to come—is that quality of life characterized by showing mercy for those in need, regardless of their race, religion, or region—and with no thought of reward.[9]

Imagine the shock of the story's plot twist for the religious leader who originally asked Jesus the question about who was his neighbor. He must have still been sorting through his own offended emotions when Jesus turned to him and said:

> "Now which of these three would you say was a neighbor to the man who was attacked by bandits?" Jesus asked.
> The man replied, "The one who showed him mercy."
> Then Jesus said, "Yes, now go and do the same." (Luke 10:36-37, NLT)

WHO was the neighbor? Now Jesus is asking the questions. WHO is *your* neighbor? Jesus is relentless. The religious leader can't even bring himself to say the words "the Samaritan" in response. The idea destabilizes everything he believes in. All he can do to answer Jesus is to describe him as "the one who showed him mercy."

But Jesus isn't finished with him yet. He adds injury to insult. He tells this religious Jew who now stands in front of him that he must go beyond being open to seeing Samaritans as neighbors. He must make all those who live a life of love, regardless of their race or religion, his example to follow.

It was not easy to play the role of the Good Samaritan in this story. He invested his time and his money in helping the wounded man. He turned his ass into an ambulance and gave up his personal agenda for the rest of the day. He also ran the risk of being attacked himself. Who knows, the bandits could still have been close by. The man at the side of the road could have been one of them—a kind of decoy, bandit bait. This road between Jericho and Jerusalem was known for its danger at the time of Jesus.[10] But the Samaritan let go of his personal "to-do list," his hard-earned money, and even his own safety in order to show love to a stranger.

The way of Jesus is the way of risky love. Religion is the way of safety, security, and shelter within the structure of rules, regulations, rituals, and routines. Jesus and his earliest followers were relentless in pressing people to see two things. First, loving people is the primary way we love God (see Matthew 25:31-46; John 14:15,21,23; James 2:8-18; 1 John 4:20-21; 5:3; 2 John 6). Second, this love of humankind must always take precedence over religious ritual or ethnic obstacles (see Matthew 5:23-24; John 10:16; Galatians 3:28).

Think for a moment on the scandalous implications of this story for our own day and way of living. Even among Christ-followers I regularly find that people squirm, both intellectually and emotionally, to try to wriggle out of the clear closing injunction of Christ: "Go and do the same." "But you have to be wise," is a favorite comeback. Well, wisdom is good, but love is even better. And Christ-followers are called to be, according to the standards of this world, "foolish" (1 Corinthians 1:20-31; 4:10). Real love is, from a purely human, self-serving perspective, irrational.

Jesus is laying down a principle that has implications for everyone at all times—especially those who want to pursue a spiritually healthy life. He warns us that religious traditions can be a trap that keeps us from moving into uncharted territories of bold love and radical compassion. Irreligious people, on the other hand, are free to be more loving.[11] Jesus calls people to love in such a way that all social barricades are broken, penetrated, subverted—including and especially those erected by religion. And to love like God wants, we must be willing to put practical service ahead of safety, comfort, and convenience.

Again, to quote Alan Culpepper,

> To love God with all one's heart and one's neighbor as oneself meant then and now that one must often reject society's rules in favor of the codes of the kingdom—a society without distinctions and boundaries between its members. The rules of that society are just two—to love God and one's neighbor—but these rules are so radically different from those of the society in which we live that living by them invariably calls us to disregard all else, break the rules, and follow Jesus' example.[12]

Jesus challenges the strong kinship-based identity of first-century Israel by offering a radical reorientation of family values:

> "Who are my mother and my brothers?" he asked.
> Then he looked at those seated in a circle around him and said, "Here are my mother and my brothers! Whoever does God's will is my brother and sister and mother." (Mark 3:33-35)

Through these words, Jesus opposes the idea that birth, blood, and biology define true family. Instead, he stresses that our unity with God and one another comes through shared faith and common purpose. In this way, Jesus invites his followers to become part of a worldwide, transnational, multiethnic family of faith. And so, it is to his Jewish friends that Jesus says, "I have other sheep that do not belong to this fold. I must bring them also, and they will listen to my voice. So there will be one flock, one shepherd" (John 10:16, NRSV).

The apostle Paul describes the inclusive reality of the kingdom this way: "There is no longer Jew or Greek, there is no longer slave or free, there is no longer male and female; for all of you are one in Christ Jesus. And if you belong to Christ, then you are Abraham's offspring, heirs according to the promise" (Galatians 3:28-29, NRSV). And again: "In this new life, it doesn't matter if you are a Jew or a Gentile, circumcised or uncircumcised, barbaric, uncivilized, slave, or free. Christ is all that matters, and he lives in all of us" (Colossians 3:11, NLT).

In Christ's kingdom, ethnicity, social status, or gender identity are no longer important categories of distinction. Instead, all members of this kingdom are unified as one family, with God as our shared Father and Abraham as our shared ancestor. The early Christ-followers, although wildly diverse in ethic origins and socioeconomic status, called each other "brother" and "sister." This was not as a form of polite rhetoric or friendly posturing, but a way to express a deep *reality* they believed Jesus brought about—a new society of radical inclusivity, a sociological miracle that up until that time no one believed was possible.

Think for a moment about the many horrors of the past that have grown out of ethnic loathing, nationalistic selfishness, and religious tribalism. Think about whatever stories of hatred, brutality, and war are currently in the news. What human hostilities in the world today are the offspring of racial revulsion, economic oppression, or gender discrimination? Think of how our world would be different if people embraced this one teaching of Jesus: We are all family.

When we realize this agenda of Jesus, many of his offensive teachings begin to make sense. When Jesus tells people to be prepared to "hate" their families in Luke 14:26 (uh-huh, he says that, really), he is preparing people obsessed with kinship identity for life in a new kind of society where everyone is welcomed as "family."[13] One by one, Jesus helps people "unplug" from the things they may personally benefit from but that get in the way of achieving radically diverse unity. For any one individual to embrace this inclusive way of Jesus would mean the possibility of being rejected and scorned by family and friends. This puts each person into a position of existential choice—a pure, individual decision—beyond the system in which he or she exists. So Jesus says things like, "Do not think that I came to bring peace on the earth; I did not come to bring peace, but a sword" (Matthew 10:34, NASB), and he says this in the context of discussing family ties. The emphasis in context is not on dividing families, but on freeing individuals to make their own choices of faith. Our spiritual convictions should not be mandated for us because of the genetics or geography of our birth.

Q & Eh?

1. Who is a "Samaritan" to you (not in the sense of being a "Good Samaritan," but just a Samaritan, as the term would have meant to a first-century Jew)? In other words, to whom do you feel superior? Whom do you secretly (or not so secretly) despise? Try to answer with brutal self-searching honesty. Even if you do not *want* to feel superior to these people, ask yourself if you do feel superior to:

Liberals	Conservatives
Rich people	Poor people
Politicians	Police officers
Criminals	Lawyers
Physically challenged people	Physically superior people

Mentally challenged people	Mentally superior people
Garbage collectors	Golfers
Truck drivers	Taxi drivers
Slow drivers	Tailgaters
Artists	Scientists
Socialists	Capitalists
Welfare recipients	Public servants
Telemarketers	Televangelists
Feminists	Traditionalists
Homemakers	Home wreckers
Homosexuals	Heterosexuals
Transsexuals	Metrosexuals
Students	Teachers
Street people	Sales people
Religious people	Atheists
Blacks	Whites
Reds	Yellows
Blondes	Brunettes
Jews	Arabs
Men	Women
Adults	Children
Adult children	Childish adults
Therapists	People who are in therapy
People who should be in therapy	People who put you in therapy
Attractive people	Ugly people
Famous people	Family members
Fat people	Skinny people
Dog people	Cat people
Vegetarians	Omnivores
Conformists	Anarchists
Hippies	Yuppies
Virgins	Sooo-not-virgins
People who drink	People who don't drink

| People who drive you to drink | People who like country music |
| People who like Monty Python | People who don't like Monty Python |

Now try to recast the parable of the Pharisee and the tax collector in Luke 18:9-14 to fit your life situation. Read it closely and think it through. Then pray—and decide which prayer you want to make your own.

2. In the story of the Good Samaritan, three attitudes toward material goods are demonstrated: (a) *The thieves*—"What's yours is mine, and I'm going to get it"; (b) *The religious leaders*—"What's mine is mine, and I'm going to keep it"; (c) *The Samaritan*—"What's mine is yours, and I'm going to share it." Ask yourself honestly, when do you play the role of each in your life?

———❖———

There is no longer Jew or Greek, there is no longer slave or free,
there is no longer male and female; for all of you are one in Christ Jesus.
And if you belong to Christ, then you are Abraham's
offspring, heirs according to the promise.

— GALATIANS 3:28-29, NRSV

———❖———

CHAPTER TEN

Thy Kingdom Come

Transcending Territory

*[Jesus] is not concerned to attack existing economic or political
institutions. . . . The revolution he sought was a far deeper one,
without which reforms could only be superficial and transitory.
If he could cleanse the human heart of selfish desire, cruelty, and
lust, utopia would come of itself, and all those institutions that
rise out of the human greed and violence, and the consequent
need for law, would disappear.*

— WILL DURANT

Many religions tend to focus on the afterlife and how to prepare for it.
Our life now can end up being reduced to a kind of dress rehearsal, a
place to prepare for the real life to come.

The religious fixation on salvation as an otherworldly destination
allows for frustrating disconnects between this life and the next. For
instance, Hindus can ignore the basic needs of the hurting lower castes
while they look forward to eventually entering a state where everyone's
needs and desires are met. Muslims teach marital fidelity and abstinence
from alcohol in this life while they anticipate the heavenly rewards of
multiple virginal sex partners and rivers flowing with wine in the next

life. Christians fight wars in order to spread peace and may ignore the environmental issues of our planet because heaven is all that matters.

But Jesus invites us to live one unending and coherent life, starting *now*. He calls for continuity between how we want to live for all eternity and how we actually live in the present. Jesus raises the question: Are you living now the way you want to live forever?

Without the continuous, one-life spirituality of Jesus, religion can produce a kind of end-justifies-the-means spirituality, where judgmental intolerance and "defensive" violence are completely accepted in this life as we prepare for an afterlife of peace and harmony. It was this kind of compartmentalization that made it possible for Christians to torture heretics in order to save their souls and still allows zealous Muslims to blow themselves and others up in order to enter a heavenly reward. Violence as a road to peace? Jesus says there is a better way.

In one sense, we could say that belief in God has intensified rather than alleviated a fundamental human problem. Humans have different opinions, different cultures, different approaches to life, different earthly "kingdoms" that we are already willing to argue, fight, and kill for. Belief that God is on our side only increases the zeal. Once people believe that their opinions are God-sanctioned, the cause for which they were already willing to fight takes on cosmic significance. It's as if belief in God injects our zeal for a cause with supernatural steroids. Wherever faith in God is strong, our human predisposition for using violence to enforce what we believe is right will only increase. This was as true for the medieval church as it is for many contemporary Muslims. This is why theistic faith must be partnered with a clear commitment to peace as a way of life if our faith is to be constructive rather than destructive. Jesus couldn't be clearer on this topic.

The spirituality of Jesus does not allow for the separation of means and ends. Jesus doesn't view peace as a goal to be achieved by any means necessary (à la Malcolm X). Peace is not just a goal to be achieved, but a lifestyle to be lived. This is because, as Dallas Willard and Don Simpson point out in their book, *Revolution of Character* (Colorado

Springs: NavPress, 2005), the emphasis of Jesus' spirituality is not on getting us into the realm of heaven, but bringing the qualities of heaven into our daily experiences on earth. When Christ-followers realize this, the separation of the goal and the means to reach that goal disappears. In the words of Martin Luther King Jr., "Peace is not merely a distant goal that we seek, but a means by which we arrive at that goal."[1]

What life do you want to live for all eternity? If a life of peace and love and joy and unity is your ultimate goal, then start living out these realities *now*. When we live now the way God wants us to live forever, we are welcoming his kingdom, his loving authority, his way of living into our world.

As you read Jesus' teaching, you cannot help but notice the recurring theme of the "kingdom of God" or "kingdom of heaven." In fact, his entire message is summarized as "the good news of the kingdom" (Matthew 4:23; 9:35; Luke 4:43, NRSV). Most of his parables are simple illustrations of this one reality (see Matthew 13). Embedded within this kingdom message is an invitation or challenge to his listeners. Jesus says, "The time is fulfilled, and the kingdom of God has come near; repent, and believe in the good news" (Mark 1:15; NRSV).

The kingdom of God, according to Jesus, is not a realm we enter when we die but a way of life we can choose to enter now. Jesus taught his followers to pray, "Your kingdom come. Your will be done, on earth as it is in heaven" (Matthew 6:10, NASB). Every time we allow our choices to align with God's will of love for us, we experience more of his kingdom on earth. Like yeast in dough, God's kingdom begins to permeate our thoughts and attitudes and eventually our relationships, slowly transforming our lives from the inside out (see Matthew 13:33; Luke 13:20-21).

Some religionists do focus on how to bring God's kingdom to earth—but they miss the nature of what that kingdom should look like. These religious devotees tend to see God's kingdom on earth as a political structure that blends faith with force. Think of nations today under Muslim rule (sharia law) or medieval Christian nations or the ancient

Roman practice of emperor worship, where religion and politics are just two aspects of the same substance. Think of how this principle of politicization of faith plays out in contemporary American politics, regardless of how much Americans verbalize the ideal of "separation of church and state." In these kinds of kingdoms, those with power (whether military power, lobbying power, financial power, or voting power) enforce their interpretation of God's will rather than allow people the freedom to pursue God's will out of a desire to know God intimately.

This is not unlike the culture into which Jesus first came. In Jesus' world the lines between nationality, ethnicity, and religion were somewhere between fuzzy and nonexistent. For instance, was being "Jewish" a way of referring to one's ethnicity, nationality, or religion? The answer was simply "yes," and separating these concepts would have seemed foreign, even sacrilegious, to Jesus' peers.

Into this cultural landscape, Jesus injected a completely new way of thinking about being a part of a kingdom. By "kingdom," he is not talking about a political structure but a realm of relationships where God's way of love is upheld and experienced. To be a part of the kingdom of God (or kingdom of heaven, as it is sometimes called) is to enter a whole new way of living where we submit to and partner with God's loving ways at work in the world, no matter what earthly kingdom we might also belong to.

Think of it this way—we all have a "kingdom." Our kingdom is that realm within which our will is done. A child's kingdom is small, perhaps consisting only of his or her own toys, and even then Mom and Dad sometimes pull rank and make the child put the toys away. As we grow older, our own personal kingdom expands, and we have more say over our own destiny. But we must still learn how to live within and submit to other authority structures—the kingdom of family, of school, of work, and the kingdom of our nation. At the same time, we can choose to live within and to help expand the kingdom of God—that realm within which *his* will is done. Whenever we willingly follow the teaching of Jesus, choosing his way of love over our temptation to be self-serving, we are helping bring the kingdom of God to earth—a sphere of living in which God's will of love is consistently embraced and applied.

From this point of view, every Christ-follower has a kind of dual citizenship. For instance, I am Canadian, but I am also a citizen of God's kingdom on earth, his "holy nation" (1 Peter 2:9). Through our shared citizenship in this spiritual kingdom, those who follow the way of Jesus on earth become partners in bringing peace, regardless of nationality. Whenever our earthly kingdom calls us to participate in something that is not aligned with our heavenly kingdom, we are placed in a position of choice.

As you might imagine, this understanding can place us in positions of creative tension with our earthly kingdoms in a variety of ways. My corporate-career kingdom may tell me that profit is the bottom line, but God's kingdom tells me that I am called to help care for creation and not exploit the poor. My national kingdom may call me to go to war, to kill others in the name of national defense; but the kingdom of God tells me to love my enemies and to respond to violence with blessing. The question becomes, in these times of tension, which kingdom rules supreme in the lives of those who claim to follow Jesus?

The kingdom teaching of Jesus has huge ramifications for our approach to the issue of violence and war. Understandably, an earthly kingdom cannot endure without the use of violence. In our world, countries would not survive without at least the threat of force within (police) and without (army). But what about the kingdom of Christ?

Religions have a history of taking their cues from political kingdoms rather than offering an alternate approach to life. Whether that be Tibetan Buddhism, Islamic rule, medieval Christianity, or ancient Judaism, the idea of a certain land or ethnicity or political structure or rule of law being uniquely sacred has led to a fractured planet.

It was into a world with this religious-political focus that Jesus introduced an entirely new concept of what God's kingdom would look like when it comes upon the earth. It would not be a political structure or an institutional edifice, but the simple rule of God in human hearts, uniting them together in loving community, regardless of their earthly kingdom allegiances. In Jesus' day, Israel was an occupied nation under Roman rule. They longed for God to send them a Messiah, a king like David, who would lead them in battle against the Romans, destroy their enemies, and establish his kingdom in their land. So when Jesus taught his followers to pray for God's kingdom to come upon the earth (see Matthew 6:10) this could have been considered a code for rebellion against the current power structures. In fact, this is exactly what it was, but not in the ways people expected.

Instead of teaching his followers how to fight against the Romans, Jesus taught them how to love their enemies. He said that if a Roman soldier commanded them to carry his gear one mile, they should obey the command, and then offer to carry it a second mile (see Matthew 5:38-47; Luke 6:27-36). The first mile is slavery. The second mile is freedom. That is the liberating power of enemy-love.

When Jesus was brought before him for interrogation, the Roman governor Pilate asked Jesus if he was indeed trying to establish a rival kingdom. Jesus' answer to this question would be important to Pilate, since Rome didn't take kindly to rival kingdom movements. Jesus informs Pilate, "My kingdom is not of this world," and then adds, "if it were, my servants would fight" (John 18:36). The distinguishing mark of citizenship in Christ's kingdom, says Jesus to Pilate, is that members of his kingdom do not fight.[2]

This one point explains so much about why the teachings of Jesus can seem at odds with the Old Testament patterns of violence. According to the Bible, in the Old Testament days, God's kingdom on earth was rooted in ancient Israel—a people group who became a *nation*. This was a *political* kingdom with a *geographical* base, which meant that armies were needed to fight in order to establish and preserve borders.

In the New Testament, God's kingdom is described as a *spiritual* kingdom made up of people from every tribe and nation. There are still wars to fight, but they are spiritual wars against a spiritual enemy (see Ephesians 6:10-18). People, even evil people, are never seen as the enemy but as victims of the real Enemy. They are in need of rescue, not judgment. This fresh perspective has the power to radically alter our approach to any form of human conflict.

So when we pray for God's kingdom to come on earth as it is in heaven, we're inviting God to rule our hearts and our relationships. Together we live as citizens of a spiritual community where, unlike political kingdoms, peace is not a goal to be obtained by any means necessary (including violence!) — peace is a way of life.[3]

This concept of God's "kingdom" being an inner reality that is lived out in our daily lives was hard for the religious leaders of Jesus' day to accept, and it has proven difficult for religious leaders to accept ever since. Throughout history, religious leaders and institutions have prostituted themselves to the state, offering divine blessing for political agendas in exchange for protection and security. Yet to all of us Jesus says we should not look for his kingdom in physical structures and organizations, for "the Kingdom of God is within you" (Luke 17:21, TEV).[4]

Jesus knew his new way of looking at God's "kingdom" would challenge the underpinnings of national and religious loyalties in his day and ours, and so within his kingdom teaching he often embeds a call to "repent":

"The time is fulfilled, and the kingdom of God has come near; repent, and believe in the good news." (Mark 1:15, NRSV)

"Repent, for the kingdom of heaven has come near." (Matthew 4:17)

To "repent" means to have a change of heart and mind, to look at things from a new point of view, to think about things differently, and to change your current course in light of the new perspective.

I once saw someone holding a sign that said, "Repent for the end is near!" He got it wrong. Jesus didn't just say the end was near. He said that the kingdom of God was near. If I repent because the end is near, then I'm just apologizing for my past in time to die and go to heaven. But if I repent because the kingdom, the Way, the rule of God is near, then I am actively deciding to change my egocentric approach to life and joining in partnership with God to help bring about his way of love in this world. I repent, not because the end is near, but because the beginning is here, and I want to be a part of it.

Christ's message of the kingdom and of our response of repentance was not just a command to regret your past, but an invitation to help bring about a new future.

Q & Eн?

1. List some examples, historical and contemporary, of religion trying to mix with politics. What are the recurring results?

2. I often hear Christians in America identify their country as a "Christian nation."

   • What do you think people who use this term mean by it?
   • Do you think this is a helpful or hurtful way of thinking about a country?

3. In Luke 6:27-28, Jesus says: "Love your enemies, do good to those who hate you, bless those who curse you, pray for those who mistreat you" (NASB).

   • What impact would it have on the world if a continually growing number of people began to live out this one simple teaching of Jesus?
   • Do you think this is just a poetic dream, or is it really possible to live out the ideal of enemy-love?

4. What do you think it would mean for you to pray "Your kingdom come. Your will be done, on earth as it is in heaven"

(Matthew 6:10, NASB)? In other words, if God answered that prayer, what would that look like in your life?

———◆◆×◆●———

"The time is fulfilled, and the kingdom of God has come near; repent, and believe in the good news."

— MARK 1:15, NRSV

———◆◆×◆●———

CHAPTER ELEVEN

Sacred Space

Redefining Temple

*Jesus was inaugurating a way of life which had
no further need of the Temple.*

— N. T. WRIGHT

Jesus lived and taught in a world that viewed life in terms of concentric circles of sacred space, which looked something like this:

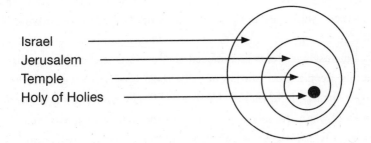

According to his religious contemporaries, although all the world belonged to God, Israel was a particularly holy land within which was Jerusalem, the holy city. In Jerusalem was the holy temple where

God's presence dwelled, animal sacrifices were offered, and forgiveness was received. And finally, within the temple was the epicenter of sacredness—the Holy of Holies, where God's presence was said to be most manifest.

Contrary to the religious norm of his day, Jesus taught a form of spirituality that erased the lines of distinction between sacred space and secular space. Accordingly, in the words of N. T. Wright, "The whole world is now seen as God's holy land."[1]

Religion bases much of its approach to life on strong distinctions between the sacred and the profane, the holy and the mundane. First it creates the distinctions, and then it offers systematic ways for people to move from one realm to the other, from the profane to the holy. Often this process includes pilgrimages to "holy" sites or attending special services in "sacred" spaces, usually special buildings that represent the institution.

Jesus upset the status quo of his day by speaking of his own body as the *temple* or *sanctuary* of God (see John 2:21)—that is, the place where the divine and human meet. Wherever he went he acted as though the divine presence was fully with him and not just back in the temple in Jerusalem.

Jesus not only communicated through direct teaching and storytelling, but through actions. His whole life amounted to what Robert Farrar Capon calls "an ambulatory parable."[2] If you want to understand Jesus, keep your eyes and ears open to what he says through what he does.

For instance, Jesus scandalized the religious leaders by personally offering people God's forgiveness for their sins. The religion of first-century Israel taught that people received God's forgiveness in a specific way—through the sacrificial system of the temple in Jerusalem. One would purchase a goat or dove from a vendor (conveniently located in the temple courts) and then present it to a priest for sacrifice. Only a priest of the temple could then conduct the ceremony and offer worshippers forgiveness of sins on behalf of God. It was quite simple, quite predictable, and all quite institutional.

Therefore, when Jesus would say to people "your sins are forgiven" (see Matthew 9:2; Luke 7:36-50), he was not just being a source of encouragement to hurting people. He was making a decidedly irreligious statement to his culture. He was completely bypassing the religious system of his day and helping people connect with God's grace, mercy, and forgiveness *directly*.

As expected, when the religious leaders heard him do this, they were understandably outraged. His actions were scandalous. What Jesus did was tantamount to thumbing his nose at the religious system. He offered people what only God *through the temple system* could offer people. He put himself in the center of God's relationship with humanity. He was saying, in effect, "Now God will forgive your sins, not through the temple, but through *me*," thereby making religion redundant. *Jesus was a one-man, walking, talking, counter-temple movement.* He now embodied all that the temple stood for. He was offering through himself what only the religious system of his day was supposed to offer—God's grace.

So offering forgiveness to sinners directly was, in a way, both a creative and destructive gesture. Creative for the human spirit; destructive for the religious system. At the same moment he was building people up, Jesus was also tearing religion down.

This Jesus-versus-temple theme reached its climax one day when Jesus visited the sacrificial institution personally. Rather than blessing it, he threw a complete temple tantrum. He turned over the tables and released all of the sacrificial animals that were used for the forgiveness ceremonies (see Matthew 21:12-14; Mark 11:15-18; Luke 19:45-48; John 2:13-17). William C. Placher writes, "If you couldn't buy the right kind of animal, then how could you sacrifice? If you couldn't sacrifice, why have a Temple? By his actions, Jesus seems to be challenging the very basis of religion."[3]

Though he shut down the system only temporarily, it was a symbolic act that called his people to rethink the whole concept of divine forgiveness and how it was applied to their lives. God never *needed* animal sacrifices to forgive.[4] Obedience without sacrifice is always better than disobedience with sacrifice.[5]

When Jesus launched this direct assault on the temple system, he explained his actions by quoting from a Hebrew prophet who had rebuked the system in his own day. Hundreds of years earlier, Jeremiah had leveled this challenge against the religious system of Israel by walking into the temple area and shouting these words:

"O Judah, listen to this message from the LORD! Listen to it, all of you who worship here! The LORD of Heaven's Armies, the God of Israel, says:

"Even now, if you quit your evil ways, I will let you stay in your own land. But don't be fooled by those who promise you safety simply because the LORD's Temple is here. They chant, 'The LORD's Temple is here! The LORD's Temple is here!' But I will be merciful only if you stop your evil thoughts and deeds and start treating each other with justice; only if you stop exploiting foreigners, orphans, and widows; only if you stop your murdering; and only if you stop harming yourselves by worshiping idols. Then I will let you stay in this land that I gave to your ancestors to keep forever.

"Don't be fooled into thinking that you will never suffer because the Temple is here. It's a lie! Do you really think you can steal, murder, commit adultery, lie, and burn incense to Baal and all those other new gods of yours, and then come here and stand before me in my Temple and chant, 'We are safe!'—only to go right back to all those evils again? Don't you yourselves admit that this Temple, which bears my name, has become a den of thieves? Surely I see all the evil going on there. I, the LORD, have spoken!" (Jeremiah 7:1-11, NLT)

A den of thieves. This was Jesus' description of the temple establishment in his own day. I used to think that because Jesus quoted Jeremiah, calling the Jerusalem temple a den of robbers, that he was upset with the institution's financial practices, charging too much money for their services and the like. But the meaning runs deeper than that. A den of robbers is not a place where thieves go to rob people, but where they go to hide out after they have done the robbing. The religious system of Israel (like any religious system today) was repeatedly used as a spiritual hideout for people with a guilty conscience. Rather than change how they lived, the people of Israel simply added a little religion to their lives to keep everything balanced. Like the godfather going to Mass on Sunday morning or going to confessional before returning to his life of crime, religious systems make it all too easy for self-centered people to find comfort in familiar rituals without experiencing a change of heart or committing to a life of love.

Like the prophets of old, Jesus challenged the status quo. But unlike the Old Covenant prophets, Jesus went further to refer to himself as the turning point, as the hinge upon which the door of change would swing. Jesus taught his followers to expect his own continuing presence to dwell, not within special buildings called "churches," but within their relationships. He said that wherever two or three people gather together in his name he would be there with them (see Matthew 18:20). If you want to get close to me, says Jesus, get close to the people I love (see Matthew 25:31-46). Jesus seems to be saying that God's presence is best experienced in the sacred space that exists between people when love is offered and received rather than in special buildings or pious places.

At first this new way of thinking was hard for his followers to grasp. They were not used to such a "portable" spirituality. One of the most striking examples of this comes from an account in Jesus' life that seems lifted from the pages of a good sci-fi novel. Some of Christ's disciples witnessed Jesus spiritually interfacing with the divine realm, as if a portal opened between the temporal and the eternal.

Peter's response to what he saw reveals the religious mentality at work. Mark's gospel describes the scene:

After six days Jesus took Peter, James and John with him and

led them up a high mountain, where they were all alone. There
he was transfigured before them. His clothes became dazzling
white, whiter than anyone in the world could bleach them. And
there appeared before them Elijah and Moses, who were talking with Jesus.

Peter said to Jesus, "Rabbi, it is good for us to be here.
Let us put up three shelters—one for you, one for Moses and
one for Elijah." (He did not know what to say, they were so
frightened.)

Then a cloud appeared and covered them, and a voice came
from the cloud: "This is my Son, whom I love. Listen to him!"

Suddenly, when they looked around, they no longer saw
anyone with them except Jesus. (Mark 9:2-8)

What a strange scene! My guess is that this was a gift from God to
Jesus in the form of a moment of deeply empowering encouragement.
Two key leaders of the Old Covenant were able to offer their blessing to
the coming of the New.

In this scene the disciples are terrified by the sight of Jesus glow-
ing while talking with two dead people. Completely understandable
—wouldn't you agree? Peter doesn't know what to say, so, in typi-
cal Peter fashion, he says whatever is on his mind anyway. (Have you
ever known someone without a "filter"?) Peter's spontaneous outburst
reveals his religious roots and echoes the general religious mindset in
the world today. A spiritual experience deserves a building, thinks Peter.
We should build a shrine. Then these three spirits will have a place to
live, and generations of people will be able to make pilgrimages to this
holy place.

But God speaks, not out of a holy building or through the lips of a
special class of religious leader—he speaks out of a cloud that refuses to
be captured by architecture or geography. Listen to Jesus, says God. He
will show you a better way.

Writer Garry Wills says, "Jesus did not come to replace the Temple with other buildings, whether huts or rich cathedrals, but to instill a religion of the heart, with only himself as the place where we encounter the Father."[6]

Taking their cues from the teaching of Jesus, the earliest Christ-followers finally came to realize that they didn't need holy buildings or special places to meet with God. They saw themselves as living stones, built together into a new organic temple, made up of the people of God. They believed that the Spirit of God dwelled within this relational temple, this sanctuary-as-community (see 1 Corinthians 3:16-17; Ephesians 2:19-22) and that their entire lives were altars upon which to offer sacrificial love to God and others (see Romans 12:1). Because of Jesus, they understood that all of life is holy and every relationship sacred. Truly, there is no holier ground than the space between you and me as we connect in honest, vulnerable, forgiving relationship.

Our Western practice of referring to church buildings as "churches" (rather than the building where a church meets) can work against our ability to see this truth. Some Christians not only call the building they meet in their "church" but they also call a special room where they hold Sunday services the "sanctuary," a word that means the sacred place where God dwells. And, to confuse our minds just a little bit more, at the front of the sanctuary is often a big table called the "altar," a word that refers to the place of animal sacrifice in Old Testament ritual. But the only altar, the only place of sacrifice Christ-followers should need, is the altar of the daily decisions of our lives, where we offer God our energies and agendas, our choices and our desires as "living sacrifice" (Romans 12:1).

This is why the early Christian movement felt no need to hold their meetings in special buildings. For about the first three hundred years, Christ-followers met primarily in people's homes (see Romans 16:5; 1 Corinthians 16:19; Colossians 4:15; Philemon 2), and may have sometimes rented a local hall for larger gatherings (see Acts 19:9-10). The idea of constructing special holy buildings called "churches" where priests would steward God's grace to the people would have been a very foreign idea to the early Christians. Instead, the early church considered every believer a priest representing God to one another (see 1 Peter 2:4-9). Even Peter, considered by some to be the first authoritative leader of the institutionalized church, simply referred to himself as a "fellow elder" along with other church leaders (1 Peter 5:1).

The word *church* in the New Testament refers to the coming together of the people, an assembly, a gathering, not a special building and not a hierarchical institution. My church, for instance, is the group of Christ-followers that I hang out with regularly and build relationships with, not the building in which we meet.[7] Together we have the privilege of being the temple, the dwelling place of God.

Q & Eh?

1. What are the (a) possible benefits and (b) possible problems of designing church buildings so that they are unique and especially glorious in their architecture and ornamentation?

2. If you believe in God:

   - In what places or circumstances do you tend to feel closer to God?
   - In what places or circumstances do you tend to feel distant from God?
   - What might be something you could do to help remind yourself of God's loving presence when you are in those places or circumstances where he feels distant?

3. As you read this, what is the most recent news about fighting over "holy land" between religions? How would our world be different if people lived out this one teaching of Jesus?

———◆▸◈◂◆———

I appeal to you therefore, brothers and sisters, by the mercies of God,
to present your bodies as a living sacrifice, holy and acceptable to God,
which is your spiritual worship.

— ROMANS 12:1, NRSV

———◆▸◈◂◆———

CHAPTER TWELVE

Subversive Symbols

*What is essential Christianity! From first to last it is scandal, the
divine scandal. Every time someone risks scandal of high order
there is joy in heaven.*

— SØREN KIERKEGAARD

When Jesus died he was relatively young, compared to other potential world-changing figures. At their respective deaths, Muhammad
was sixty, Socrates was seventy, Plato and Buddha were both more than
eighty, and Moses was one hundred twenty! Christ's death came so
comparatively early in his messianic career (probably in his early thirties) that we really only have about three years of his adult life on record.
It is amazing that he left the impact he did on human history, more than
any other figure that has ever lived.

What we know about Jesus' teaching is as bizarre as it is beautiful.
Jesus didn't just teach about God, life, and salvation; he taught about
himself, and how *he* could help us connect with God. Jesus saw himself
as a conduit to the divine. Specifically, he taught that his *death* would
somehow be the key to making that connection real (see Matthew 16:21-
25; Luke 18:31-34).

Jesus communicated his message, not only through his stories and
teachings, but also by reconfiguring significant symbols of his day.
Before he died, Jesus left his followers with two symbols of subversion,
acts of irreligion, which have survived to this day, albeit often in very
religious forms.

The first was baptism. When people went to the temple to receive for-giveness for their sin, they not only sacrificed animals, but also cleansed themselves ritually with water. They would *baptize* (from the Greek word meaning "to immerse") themselves in basins of water designed to help them wash away any spiritual impurities they had come in contact with during their daily lives. Between full-body baptisms, many reli-gious people would baptize their hands to symbolize their commitment to purity (remember the sacred jars at the wedding in Cana).

In partnership with John the Baptist, Jesus adopted this symbol but moved it away from the temple steps and into the community, wherever water was available. Baptism into the Jesus movement became a way of symbolizing that people could have their sins washed away, *apart from the religious system.* This renewed symbol did not take a special priest or pastor to administer. Instead, any spiritual brother or sister could baptize the person coming into faith as a way of partnering with him in the symbol and welcoming him into the spiritual community (see Acts 8:26-39). As well, the symbol became a single event at the outset of a person's life of faith. Recurring baptisms became unnecessary because baptism was no longer part of a system of ritualistic purification. A one-time baptism symbolized God's once-and-for-all acceptance of us. The simplicity of the symbol is beautiful. Unfortunately, many Christians use baptism today as the special ceremony that must only be adminis-tered by the paid professional holy man within the sacred space of an official "church" building. Jesus offers us a better way.

The second symbol that Jesus infused with new meaning was the Jewish Passover meal, called the *Seder.* Today Christians celebrate this reconfigured event as Communion, the Eucharist, or the Lord's Supper. At his last Passover Seder with his disciples, Jesus infused the event with new meaning, designed to help us all understand the significance of his death and our response of faith. Just hours before his arrest and crucifixion, Jesus found a way to explain its meaning to his disciples in a way they would never forget (Matthew 26:17-30; Mark 14:12-26; Luke 22:7-23). Through this last supper Jesus was also able to leave all future generations a way of commemorating and recalibrating their lives around the centrality of his death.

> For I received from the Lord that which I also delivered to you, that the Lord Jesus in the night in which He was betrayed took bread; and when He had given thanks, He broke it and said, "This is My body, which is for you; do this in remembrance of Me." In the same way He took the cup also after supper, saying, "This cup is the new covenant in My blood; do this, as often as you drink it, in remembrance of Me." For as often as you eat this bread and drink the cup, you proclaim the Lord's death until He comes. (1 Corinthians 11:23-26, NASB)

How telling that the Lord's Supper, which is the only ongoing commemorative act authorized by Jesus, dramatizes not his birth or life, words or works, but only his death and resurrection (hey, you do get to come out of the water too, right?). Obviously Jesus wanted his crucifixion to become the fulcrum of his followers' faith. But why?

The Passover Seder was not a neutral meal to begin with. Already it was the symbolic celebration of liberation from bondage, achieved through the shedding of blood. Long ago, God had liberated Israel from their slavery in Egypt, and the Passover meal celebrated this fact. The death of the firstborn, the blood of the animal sacrifices, and the freedom these things achieved for the Israelites were all embedded elements in this meal of remembrance. It is within this context, a celebration of a miraculous freedom, that Jesus calls the bread "my body, which is given for you" (Luke 22:19, NRSV) and the wine "my blood which is the new agreement that God makes with his people." Then he adds, "This blood is poured out for many to forgive their sins" (Matthew 26:28, NCV).

A new covenant. A new agreement between God and us. A new way of experiencing God. A new means to receive forgiveness. A new opportunity for renewed relationship with our Creator. All offered apart from the established religious structure.

Through the newly invigorated symbolism of the Last Supper, Jesus shows his disciples what would replace the blood of the sacrificial system—Jesus' own blood. Jesus had condemned the temple system, and now he offers himself as the replacement, the final sacrifice that would make all other sacrifices trivial. Jesus claims to have successfully replaced religion with himself.

I think that last sentence is worth unpacking. Jesus claims to have successfully replaced religion with *himself.* Not with a new system of priests and sacrifices. This is important. The symbolic meal to which Jesus invites us repeatedly points to Jesus himself as the way to God, not a new institution (the church) that replaces the old institution (the temple), not a new system of priests that replaces the old system of priests. Through Jesus, God replaces religion with himself.

So today we eat the bread and drink from the cup for one reason—the reason Jesus gave us—to remember him, to bring our focus back to everything Jesus has accomplished. This is the purpose of Communion. We do this not to receive forgiveness through a ritual. Forgiveness is already ours. We do not receive God by coming to a priest who alone can make the miracle happen. God has come to us and has bypassed all the priests and prophets in the process. We take part in the Eucharist, the Lord's Supper, to remember, to recalibrate our thinking, to bring our minds back again to the subversive message of Jesus. "Do this in remembrance of me."

What about Jesus should we "remember" through the Eucharist? Well, now it gets interesting. In order to answer that question, I want us to appreciate the shock value in the symbol. Try to put yourself in the disciples' place, as though you were hearing this for the first time. Jesus is asking his followers to mime the consumption of his corpse. No matter how you slice it (pardon the pun), that is just plain weird. But it gets worse. Jesus is very specific—he says they are to drink his blood.

Jesus alluded to this idea of eating his flesh and drinking his blood once before in his teaching career, and it cost him some followers (see John 6:51-66). John records, "Because of what Jesus said, many of his disciples turned their backs on him and stopped following him" (John 6:66, CEV). You would think Jesus should have learned his lesson — scrap the whole "drink my blood" message.

But rather than rethink, repackage, reshape his symbolism into something a little less offensive, Jesus turns up the volume on his macabre message. He doesn't just talk about it; he invites his disciples to physically participate with him in acting out this emblematic and irreligious teaching.

Let's be clear about this. If there is one thing you shouldn't ask a group of young Jewish men to do, it is drink blood. It doesn't matter whether it is human or animal, real or symbolic. The Hebrew Bible commands against ingesting blood in any fashion. This is an unambiguous rule. Meat must be drained, blood must be avoided:

> "And if any native Israelite or foreigner living among you eats or drinks blood in any form, I will turn against that person and cut him off from the community of your people, for the life of the body is in its blood. I have given you the blood on the altar to purify you, making you right with the LORD. It is the blood, given in exchange for a life, that makes purification possible. That is why I have said to the people of Israel, 'You must never eat or drink blood — neither you nor the foreigners living among you.'" (Leviticus 17:10-12, NLT)

Asking his disciples to enact the drinking of his blood does more than merely offend their sensibilities: It is a direct dismantling of religious rules in favor of radical allegiance to Jesus. He is placing his disciples in the position of making a choice. To participate in a Passover meal with redefined symbols that intentionally conflict with biblical law is sacrilege. From this point on there will be no turning back. Jesus is not giving his followers the option of simply adding his teaching to their already established religious beliefs. He is not inviting us to use his spiritual insights as a kind of seasoning to perk up our current bland religious diets. There is no room for syncretism, for blending a bit of Jesus with a bit of religious tradition as our path to God. Jesus invites the disciples to unplug from their religious identity so they can be fully engaged in their commitment to his new way.

This call to exclusivity is not unlike any marriage commitment. A single person cannot simply "add" marriage to their already established life. Marriage, if it is to be properly understood and embraced, changes our lives in profound ways. Jesus does not function like a kind of spiritual consultant that we can hire to help us do a slightly better job in our current religious practices. He is a lover calling us to embrace him in an exclusive, committed, passionate relationship—a relationship with God himself that will make all other affiliations infinitely secondary.

Of course, the more rich and wonderful one's religious heritage, the more difficult it becomes to leave it behind for Jesus. The more admirable our religious roots, the more we will want to simply invite Jesus to join our religion. We become like a young woman who loves her family of origin so much that she wants her new husband to simply move in and become another family member rather than help her establish her own home. People from a proudly labeled "Christian" background may have the most trouble with the delicate work of separating Christian culture from Christ. Christians can be the worst for inviting Jesus to bless their religious and political agendas rather than submitting everything they are to his radical way of living.

It might be helpful for us to place ourselves in the disciples' emotional shoes for a moment. When Jesus invites them to drink his blood, a gesture that breaks ties with their most cherished religious rules and rituals, what do you think ran through their heads? I can imagine Thomas looking over to John and wondering, *Is he really going to drink it?* So many questions must have flooded into the moment. Do they continue with the Passover as Jesus is redefining it, or do they leave the meal and the movement in protest? Are they willing to follow Jesus all the way, knowing he is leading them out of the safety zone of religion and into uncharted spiritual territory? Are they finally willing to take it all—the redefined Passover, the crucified Messiah, the way of life through death and freedom through sacrifice—into themselves by drinking the wine of the New Covenant? Or will they go back to the safety of their religious traditions?

These are the questions Christ-followers and potential Christ-followers must still wrestle with. Jesus intentionally puts all of us in a position of decision. Will we reject all systems of salvation in favor of trusting his irreligious way?

Think of the role our choice plays in these subversive symbols. Although some Christian denominations baptize infants today, this was not the practice in the days of Jesus or the earliest Christ-followers. Baptism was a symbol of personal choice demonstrating our desire to be plunged into the love and life of God, or "into Christ" (Galatians 3:27). And at the Last Supper, Jesus could have made his point by breaking the bread and placing it back on the table for all to see. "Look at it," he could have said. "This is my body, broken for you." Next, he could have taken the cup of wine and poured it out on the floor saying, "This is my blood, poured out for you." It would have been a vivid illustration of Christ's sacrifice (although it would have made for rather messy communion services in most churches today, but that's not my point). Instead, Jesus invites us to take the bread and wine *inside* ourselves. *We* have a role to play. Jesus offers us his life and his love, but this is not something done for us or to us while we passively observe.[1] We must embrace it.

Intimacy. That is what comes to mind when I think of these symbols. Through baptism we enter and are surrounded by God's love. Through the Lord's Supper, we invite his love and life to enter and refresh us. We are plunged into divine love and we drink it in.

Q & Eн?

1. What was your understanding of Christian baptism and Eucharist while growing up? How is that changing, if at all?

2. What are some ways that Jesus' original intent for these symbols is in conflict with how they are often used today in the Christian religion?

3. What is the role of "choice" in these symbols? How is that different from the Old Testament or Jewish Covenant?

———◆◆◆◆◆———

Some of us are Jews, and others are Gentiles. Some of us are slaves, and others are free. But God's Spirit baptized each of us and made us part of the body of Christ. Now we each drink from that same Spirit.

— 1 CORINTHIANS 12:13, CEV

———◆◆◆◆◆———

CHAPTER THIRTEEN

The Day Religion Died

I often wonder if religion is the enemy of God.
It's almost like religion is what happens when the
Spirit has left the building.

— BONO

Jesus didn't just die; he was executed. The Christian faith is unique among major world religions in that its founder was executed by established authority.[1]

Who killed Christ? Attempts to answer this question are usually misplaced, for the question itself shifts the focus away from the *self-*sacrificial nature of Christ's death, which Jesus himself emphasizes.

Sometimes Jesus spoke of his own death in cryptic symbolism: "Very truly, I tell you, unless a grain of wheat falls into the earth and dies, it remains just a single grain; but if it dies, it bears much fruit" (John 12:24, NRSV).

Many times, he plainly points to his own death as the focal point of his mission:[2] "For even the Son of Man came not to be served but to serve others and to give my life as a ransom for many" (Mark 10:45, NLT; also see Matthew 16:21-25; Mark 9:31; 10:32-34; Luke 18:31-33).

Yet throughout history many people, usually devout Christians, have tried to find someone else to blame, which usually ends up being the Jews. Others defend the Jews by pointing to the Romans—after all, Jesus was *crucified*, a distinctly Roman form of capital punishment. Some people blame individuals, like the Roman governor Pilate, or Caiaphas the high priest, or Judas Iscariot, while others (such as the writer of the Gnostic gospel of Judas) seek to absolve Judas of any responsibility. Others take a more theological approach, blaming God for the murder of his Son (who wants a parent like *that*?), while others defend God by pointing to Satan as the instigator of Jesus' death.

Jesus, however, claims responsibility for his own death: "No one can take my life from me. I sacrifice it voluntarily" (John 10:18, NLT).

Nevertheless, from a historical perspective, some people might still argue that we should blame the Jews for rejecting Jesus or the Romans for crucifying him. This is an adventure in missing the point. If we want to look beyond Jesus himself to find blame, we should look to the institutions that he threatened, not the ethnic groups of his day. To be clear, the biblical record suggests that the majority of common people (mostly Jews, but also some Samaritans and Romans) who heard Jesus were at least fans if not followers. The Gospels record that Jesus drew crowds of thousands. It was his growing *popularity* that motivated the religious leaders to find a way to have Jesus secretly arrested and tried. In his masterful book *What Jesus Meant*, Pulitzer Prize–winning author Garry Wills writes, "The most striking, resented, and dangerous of Jesus' activities was his opposition to religion as that was understood in his time. This is what led to his death. Religion killed him."[3]

Religion killed Christ. Or, I might add, religion partnered with politics. History shows that when religious and political establishments come together for a cause, it often involves violence, war, and death.

Still, we must not forget the fact that Jesus saw his own death on a Roman cross as the center of his mission. It was *his* plan all along—a plan of rescue and victory, even though it might look like utter defeat. This leads us to ask, what precisely happened on the cross for Jesus and his followers to view it as the single most significant event in history?[4] If we look beyond the nails, the wood, and the blood, what do we see?

It seems absurd that the public execution of a Jewish peasant some two thousand years ago should have any bearing on our spiritual lives today. Certainly, the cross has become a symbol of faith for many people around the world, but it is a strange symbol for any spiritual group to make their own. Buddhists have the lotus flower. Our Jewish friends use the Star of David. Islam is often symbolized by a crescent moon. Why would Christians use what is basically a symbol of ancient, agonizing capital punishment as our rallying sign?

I wonder: If Jesus came today and died at the hands of one of our governments, would Christians now be using an electric chair or a lethal injection syringe as their spiritual symbol of choice? Oh, that would be interesting. Would we adorn church buildings with electric chairs and wear smaller versions around our necks? Perhaps some believers would prefer silver electric chairs, some gold, and some would like "the old rugged electric chair" version, made out of wood complete with leather straps and metal plates. Of course, Catholics and Protestants would find new ways to argue over their symbol usage, since Catholics would actually have the figure of a person sitting in their electric chair and Protestants would keep theirs empty.

Such morbid musings raise the question of why Christians began to use the cross as a symbol of their faith. They not only drew, painted, and engraved the cross as a pictorial symbol of their faith, but they also made the sign of the cross on themselves regularly. They could have chosen a manger or a shepherd's staff or a stone like the one that was rolled away from Christ's empty tomb. They could have continued to use the sign of the fish, a dove, or an athlete's victory palm as the earliest generations of Christians did.

We must ask ourselves: How is it possible that the early Christians could think of the crucifixion of their Messiah as "good news" (the meaning of *gospel*)? How did the first generation of Christians take such a horrific event and turn it into a good news message?

On the surface, the crucifixion of Jesus looks like a photographic negative. The dark is light, death is life, and a Jewish prisoner of Rome is offering everyone else freedom. But the first followers of Jesus were convinced that this event, the death of their leader, was the doorway into a whole new world. This was a world without religion where all people could access God's grace and experience his presence directly, just as only the most holy of priests and prophets had done before. They were convinced that, if Jesus was the door into this completely new way of living, the cross was the hinge upon which the door swung.

When Jesus drew his final breath on the cross, his followers claimed that something happened that would forever signal the end of religion. In the temple in Jerusalem was a large heavy curtain, a veil that separated the rest of the temple from the Most Holy Place. The Holy of Holies was where God's presence was believed to dwell in undiluted majesty. At one time, this was the place where the ark of the covenant was kept, but since invaders had carried it away, nothing remained but an empty space made holy by God's glorious presence. No one ever went into the Holy of Holies except the high priest, and he entered only once a year to make atonement for the sins of Israel. Nothing could better symbolize the dividing line between the sacred and the profane, the holy and the mundane, than the veil of the temple. It was a line drawn in the sand, with God on one side and everyone else on the other.[5]

At the moment of Jesus' death, the Bible records that the veil of the temple was torn in two—from top to bottom (see Matthew 27:51; Mark 15:38; Luke 23:45). God himself seems to have stepped into the picture and confirmed the message and mission of Jesus through his own act of irreligious "vandalism." The dividing wall between those who are "in" and those who are "out" was finally done away with.

> For Christ himself has brought peace to us. He united Jews and Gentiles into one people when, in his own body on the cross, he broke down the wall of hostility that separated us. He did this by ending the system of law with its commandments and regulations. He made peace between Jews and Gentiles by creating in himself one new people from the two groups. (Ephesians 2:14-15, NLT)

By his death, Jesus ended the whole system of religious law that kept Jews and Gentiles separated. Jesus somehow absorbed into himself the whole system of rules and rituals that mediated between God and people, and through his death, he nailed it all to the cross: "He canceled the debt, which listed all the rules we failed to follow. He took away that record with its rules and nailed it to the cross." (Colossians 2:14, NCV)

Yes, the Bible says that Jesus died for our sins.[6] But it also says he died for our religion. In Christ, God crucified the whole mess once and for all. In fact, by repeatedly emphasizing that Jesus died for our sins, the biblical writers were emphasizing the end of religion as a way to God. Theologian Marcus Borg explains:

> According to temple theology, certain kinds of sins and impurities could be dealt with only through sacrifice in the temple. Temple theology thus claimed an institutional monopoly on the forgiveness of sins; and because the forgiveness of sins was a prerequisite for entry into the presence of God, temple theology also claimed an institutional monopoly on access to God.
>
> In this setting, to affirm "Jesus is the sacrifice for sin" was to deny the temple's claim to have a monopoly on forgiveness and access to God. It was an anti-temple statement. Using the metaphor of sacrifice, it subverted the sacrificial system. It meant: God in Jesus has already provided the sacrifice and has thus taken care of whatever you think separates you from God; you have access to God apart from the temple and its system of sacrifice. It is a metaphor of radical grace, of amazing grace. . . . It is therefore ironic to realize that the religion that formed around Jesus would within four hundred years begin to claim for itself an institutional monopoly on grace and access to God.[7]

We no longer need to imagine that God dwells in special places like sanctuaries, church buildings, temples, or tabernacles. Nor is he

156 THE END OF RELIGION

accessed only through special holy men, like priests and pastors, rabbis and imams. The final sacrifice has been offered. It's time to move along. The show is over. God has left the building.

Q & Eн?

1. How would you answer the question, Who is responsible for the death of Christ?

2. Speaking of his own death, Jesus said, "Very truly, I tell you, unless a grain of wheat falls into the earth and dies, it remains just a single grain; but if it dies, it bears much fruit" (John 12:24, NRSV). What kind of fruit do you think Jesus was hoping his death would produce?

3. The Bible speaks of Jesus dying to shut down religion but also to show us God's love and to save us from sin. What are the implications of saying that the death of Jesus:

   • shows us God's love (see Luke 15:11-32; John 3:16-17; Romans 5:8);
   • saves us from sin (see Matthew 9:1-8; John 1:29; 12:46-47; Ephesians 2:5; 1 Timothy 1:15);
   • shuts down religion (John 17:3; Romans 10:4; Ephesians 2:14-15; 1 Timothy 2:5)?

4. Discuss (if in a group) or think about (if alone) your reaction to the following quote by John Stott:

Why am I a Christian? One reason is the cross of Christ. Indeed, I could never myself believe in God if it were not for the cross. It is the cross that gives God his credibility. The only God I believe in is the one Nietzsche (the nineteenth-century German philosopher) ridiculed as "God on the cross." In the real world of pain, how could one worship a God who was immune to it?[8]

———◆◆◆◆———

The curtain of the temple was torn in two from top to bottom.

— MARK 15:38, NASB

———◆◆◆◆———

———◆—►◄—◆———

PART THREE

THE
IRRELIGIOUS
IMPLICATIONS

———◆—►◄—◆———

*Perhaps a revolution is under way, a revolution of the Spirit
that is about to shift our core energies away from arranging life
to make it as satisfying as possible to drawing near to God. Jesus
seekers across the world are being prepared to abandon the old
way of the written code for the new way of the Spirit.*

— LARRY CRABB

CHAPTER FOURTEEN

Who Do You Think You Are — *God?*

If the life and death of Socrates were those of a sage, the life and death of Jesus were those of a God.

— JEAN-JACQUES ROUSSEAU

Nobody likes people who act as if they are the center of the universe. We've all met people like that, and we never want to meet them again.

I suppose the one exception to this could be God himself. Our relational sensitivities allow for a double standard where God is concerned because, well, he *is* the center of the universe, after all. Without him we wouldn't even be here to discuss how much we dislike arrogant, self-centered people. So God can say "worship me" or "serve me" or "do my will," and it seems appropriate because he is inviting us to center our minds and lives on the highest good. However, if anyone else gave us those kinds of messages, our response would be, "Who do you think you are — *God?*"

Our earliest and most complete record of Jesus is captured in the four existing first-century Greco-Roman biographies of Jesus, called the Gospels. In these, Jesus consistently says and does things that would lead anyone who met him today to say, "Who do you think you are — *God?*" How can someone who seems so giving, kind, and compassionate, who seems like love personified, also be so incredibly egotistical? Could it be that his sense of self-importance is somehow justified?

A couple of years ago, a spiritually searching woman asked to meet with me to discuss her questions about faith. As we sat together in a local pub, she told me that she was strangely attracted to Jesus and wanted to follow him, but she just couldn't believe that any person could somehow be God. I told her I understood the intellectual challenge, and asked her to consider the problem in reverse. Could God become a human being? "Oh sure," she said. "God can do anything." Slowly a smile spread across her face, and, as she describes it, her faith problem melted away. Her difficulty arose because she was starting at the wrong end of the equation.

As we work through the evidence and implications in this chapter, keep this in mind: The early Christians realized that the scandalous edge of their faith was not that they were attributing deity to a human being, but that they were attributing humanity to a deity. For them, the question was not, Can a man be God? but Can or would the one God, Creator of the cosmos, dare to become a man?

As we saw in part 2 of this book, Jesus had the nasty habit of offering people forgiveness for all their sins. This sounds compassionate enough, but it makes little sense if Jesus is just another prophet or teacher. By offering forgiveness for sins that did not involve him in the first place, Jesus meddled in something that should be between a person and his or her God.

I can forgive someone who offends me, and you can forgive someone who offends you. But what if you or I tried to offer forgiveness to someone who had never offended us directly? Suppose you were to walk into a home where a husband had just said something hurtful to his wife, and you said to him, "That's all right. You're forgiven." Absurd? Absolutely. You have no business forgiving someone for something that he didn't do to *you*. In fact, you would be robbing his wife of the role only she should play, for only the wounded party should decide if the offender ought to be forgiven.

What if you went for therapy to help you deal with some emotional scars left by your mother, and the therapist said, "Forgiveness is the only way to resolve the pains of the past." Of course, that would be a fine thing to say—a very "Jesus thing" to say. But what if the therapist's next move was to pick up the phone and dial your mother's house and tell her that she is forgiven and then tell you that it is all taken care of. You would be understandably outraged. Who is your therapist to forgive your mother for sins committed against *you*?

You see, we must answer the question, "Who is Jesus to offer forgiveness for every wrong done?" It seems to me that either he is an egotistical meddler in other people's business or Jesus embodies God to us in some unique way and therefore can offer forgiveness because every sin is ultimately a sin against God (see Genesis 39:9; Psalm 51:4). By saying something as audacious as "I am the way" (John 14:6) to his disciples, Jesus fundamentally challenged all of the how-to systems of the spiritual world. The way is not the Ten Commandments, the Eightfold Path, the Four Noble Truths, the Five Pillars of Action, the Six Articles of Belief, the Seven Sacraments, or any other of the systems of salvation stewarded by the religions of our planet. God himself is the way. *He* has come to earth to share this message, to show us his love, and to shut down religion once and for all. We can embrace this and the freedom it brings, or we can cling to our religious systems for the comfort and security they bring. But we cannot do both.

So what gave Jesus the right to act as he did? Who was he to reinterpret Torah, challenge tradition, undo tribalism, redefine territory, and act like he was the temple, the locus of God's presence on earth? John Stott writes, "Without a doubt the most noteworthy feature of the teaching of Jesus was its quite extraordinary self-centeredness. He was, in fact, constantly talking about himself."[1]

Stott is referring to the fact that Jesus repeatedly told parables about himself and said things like, "I am the light of the world," "I am the bread of life," "I am the way, the truth, and the life," "Come to me," and "Follow me." He even went so far as to claim that the entirety of the Hebrew Scriptures, the Old Testament of the Christian Bible, was really all about him (see John 5:39-40; Luke 24:27,44)! Stott explains further:

The prominence of the personal pronoun ("I, I, I—me, me, me") is very disturbing, especially in one who declared humility to be the pre-eminent virtue. It also sets Jesus apart from all the other religious leaders of the world. They effaced themselves, pointing away from themselves to the truth they taught; he advanced himself, offering himself to his disciples as the object of their faith, love and obedience. There is no doubt, then, that Jesus believed he was unique.[2]

We cannot avoid the fact that Jesus believed he was the instrument through whom God would bring about major changes in the spiritual landscape of planet Earth. Our earliest records of Jesus' teaching reveal an undeniable self-awareness of his unique *identity*, which is the basis for his unique *impact*.[3] For instance, in one parable, Jesus refers to other prophets and messengers of God as God's *servants*, but in the same story, he contrasts these servants with his own status as God's only *Son* (see Mark 12:1-12). Jesus was convinced that to know him was to know God (see John 8:19). When a disciple asked Jesus to show him the way to God, he gave this response:

"I am the way and the truth and the life. No one comes to the Father except through me. If you really know me, you will know my Father as well. From now on, you do know him and have seen him."

Philip said, "Lord, show us the Father and that will be enough for us."

Jesus answered: "Don't you know me, Philip, even after I have been among you such a long time? Anyone who has seen me has seen the Father. How can you say, 'Show us the Father'? Don't you believe that I am in the Father, and that the Father is in me? The words I say to you I do not speak on my own authority. Rather, it is the Father, living in me, who is doing his work." (John 14:6-10)

Here is why religion is redundant. We don't need religion as our way to God because *God* has come to *us*. He has walked among us, experiencing the pain and pleasure, the hurt and heartache of a truly human life. This is why Jesus claimed to be the *door* through which people would enter eternal life (see John 10:7-9). God is the way to life because he is the source of life, and Jesus represents God to us in human form. This also explains why the Gospels record that on at least one occasion Jesus scandalously accepts worship from someone who calls him "My Lord and my God!" (John 20:28; also see Matthew 2:11; 14:33; 28:9; 28:17; Luke 24:52; John 9:38).

In the apostle Paul's words, "God was in Christ reconciling the world to Himself" (2 Corinthians 5:19, NASB).

Because Jesus says things like "I am the way," some people are puzzled by what seems like an attitude of arrogant exclusivity in a man whom they have come to see as humble and accepting. Could Jesus be so self-important to say that no one can come to God except through him? Many people try to resolve the tension with theories about the "real" Jesus of history who is somehow very different than the Jesus described in the Bible. They keep the biblical descriptions of Jesus they like, and explain away the rest. But there is no honest historical reason to push our investigation in that direction. We need to find our answers in the texts themselves, or else we have joined ranks with the liberals and lost the ear of any religious conservatives that we want to challenge. Simply shrugging our shoulders at this point and saying, "I don't think the Jesus *I* believe in would say that" does nothing to help our search for truth or our dialogue with religious fundamentalists (see chapter 5).

So let's look the question in the face: Could Jesus really be so arrogant to say that he is the only way to God?

In one of the best-known verses of the New Testament, John 3:16, Jesus tells a Jewish religious leader about God's radical inclusivity, saying: "For God so loved the world, that He gave His only begotten Son, that *whoever* believes in Him shall not perish, but have eternal life (NASB, emphasis added).

Interestingly, some people react to this teaching by tripping over the apparent exclusivity of Jesus. Who is he to suggest that we have to believe in him to have eternal life? But when viewed in context, we see that Jesus is talking to a Jewish religious leader, a man whose ethnic origin is part and parcel with his religious identity. This is a man who is waiting for the Jewish Messiah to vindicate the Jewish people by fighting against their Roman oppressors, a man who anticipates a salvation for the Jews that will also include condemnation for their enemies. But Jesus tells this man that he has come, not to save the Jews from the Romans, but to save us all ("whoever") from our own self-destruction, our hidden (and sometimes not so hidden) sin and selfishness that eats away at us from the inside out. All he asks is that we trust him on this—that we believe in him.

The angels had announced at Jesus' birth: "Fear not: for, behold, I bring you good tidings of great joy, which shall be to all people" (Luke 2:10, KJV). Good news of great joy for all people.

You may or may not agree with Jesus' teachings, but please try to understand him first. Understanding the thrust of his message depends on our starting point—whether we look at his teachings from a human or divine starting point. If we start from our own egocentric point of view, we end up asking questions like, Why don't all religions lead equally to God? But, if we look at the Jesus story from a divine starting point, then we see the inclusive message. God came down to us in human form, embodying as well as announcing that he desires for everyone to have eternal life, apart from any one religion (see 1 Timothy 2:3-6).

This is no more exclusive than if you had fallen into a well and a rescue crew lowered down a rope as a way of escape. It would be silly to criticize their one way of escape as too exclusive or restrictive. But people often do this with God. We demand multiple options because *we* want the power to decide our own method of rescue, because *we* want to be in charge of everything. *We* want to play God. But a single solution does not imply exclusivity—not if that solution is offered to everyone without exception.

Of course, examined from a strictly human perspective, Jesus' claims about himself seem to imply an arrogant exclusivity. If any person, whether teacher, prophet, spiritual leader, or politician claimed to be the only way to God, he or she is either self-aggrandizing or self-deluded. However, if we approach the biblical teaching of Jesus in the context of the biblical story of Jesus — that God was incarnating himself through the life of Christ — then everything changes.

So when Jesus claims to be the way to the Father, he is not being arrogant. He is not setting himself up as a third party who claims to be the only one who can make the proper introductions. Read his words again in John 14:6-10 (above). Jesus claims to be the way to God because he claims to be God himself, come to meet us! When we, like Philip in the story, ask Jesus to show us God, Jesus says in effect: You're already looking at him! To know Jesus is to know God. For us then, the only way to know God is through God himself, shown to us in a knowable, observable form — in our own image!

The implication of this is world-changing. We no longer need religion to act as our intermediary, like some kind of a spiritual dating service trying to introduce us to God. God has introduced himself to us, and he has brought flowers (or chocolates, depending on how caloric you like your illustrations).

And what do we find when we meet God through Jesus? Well, ironically, he is . . . *humble.* He is the kind of God who plainly tells his disciples that he is their teacher, their Lord, and their example . . . while he washes their feet (see John 13:1-17)!

So, here is the problem for people who like to think of the historical Jesus as just a good moral teacher or wise philosopher: If we view Jesus as merely a teacher, preacher, or prophet, then we have to conclude that Jesus was incredibly arrogant and/or totally deluded about his own identity. Which raises the question: If he can't even be trusted on the matter of his own identity, why should we consider him a worthwhile teacher on any other topic?

The philosopher C. S. Lewis explains this predicament best:

> I am trying here to prevent anyone saying the really foolish thing that people often say about him: "I'm ready to accept Jesus as a great moral teacher, but I don't accept his claim to be God." That is the one thing we must not say. A man who was merely a man and said the sort of things Jesus said would not be a great moral teacher. He would either be a lunatic — on a level with the man who says he is a poached egg — or else he would be the devil of hell. You must make your choice. Either this man was, and is, the Son of God; or else a madman or something worse. You can shut him up for a fool, you can spit at him and kill him as a demon; or you can fall at his feet and call him Lord and God. But let us not come with any patronizing nonsense about his being a great human teacher. He has not left that open to us. He did not intend to.[4]

Lewis shows how the Jesus of the Bible pushes each of us to make an existential choice. The Rabbi from Nazareth forces us to either love and embrace him, or despise and reject him. But we try so hard to do neither. On the one hand, we don't want to follow him as our Lord, our Master, because we don't want to be perceived as aligning our lives with the Christian religion. Or maybe it is just that we don't like the idea of having anyone but ourselves as the master of our own destiny. Yet on the other hand, we don't want to reject Jesus as evil or deceptive. We like Jesus. We want to like Jesus. And we want him to like us, to be like us, to approve of us. But is Jesus really likeable if all along he was lying about himself, God, and the end of religion?

I cannot make sense of Jesus unless I view him as somehow God, coming to draw a line in the sand for our religion-addicted world, calling each of us to make our own choice to accept his divine embrace. Of course, once God comes to all of us directly, religion is out of a job. We can't have it both ways. Perhaps this is why Jesus said things like,

"Do you think I came to smooth things over and make everything nice? Not so. I've come to disrupt and confront!" (Luke 12:51, MSG; also see Matthew 10:34).

A few years after Jesus lived, a former religious leader who gave up everything to follow Christ wrote, "For there is one God, and there is one who brings God and human beings together, the man Christ Jesus" (1 Timothy 2:5, TEV). In their first-century context, these are some of the most spiritually subversive words in the entire Bible. They are subversive because of what they *don't* say as much as what they do say, that the one point of connection with God is *not* the accepted religious establishment of the day. The apostle Paul, formerly a religious Pharisee, concluded that his religious system of Torah observance and temple sacrifice was no longer the way to connect with God. Instead, God had come to us directly, embodied in the person of Jesus.

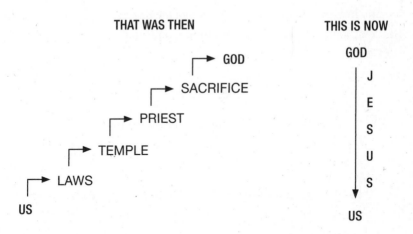

Dennis F. Kinlaw describes the world-changing wonder of this belief:

When we did not want God, God wanted us. When we would not come to God, he came to us. When we resisted him, he plotted to win us. When we could not cross the chasm that separates creation from deity, God decided to cross it and become one of us. He would not give up his deity; rather, he would unite divinity and humanity in a single person so that God and humans would really meet and become one.[5]

This message is counter to religion that offers us a set of rituals to somehow appease God. It is counter to Greek philosophy that tries to capture God in the world of theoretical ideals. And it is counter to currently popular gnostic spirituality that sees the physical world as something to be escaped from. The God that Jesus reveals to us seeks the very thing that gnostics scorn — union with the material world by means of enfleshment.

The implications are cosmic. All striving for salvation can cease. You don't have to find the right combination of religious rituals and moral behavior and enlightened understanding to please God enough to enter heaven when you die. Our eternal life begins now because God has come and, even to this day, continues to pursue us.[6]

Q & Eн?

1. Why do you think it is tempting for people to settle on the opinion that Jesus was a good moral teacher? Why is this conclusion unlikely?

2. Do you find it more difficult to believe that God could become a human being, or that any one human being could actually be God? How does our perspective change the dynamics of the discussion?

3. If God were to manifest his presence on earth in order to reveal his love to humankind, why does it make sense for him to do so in *human* form? How does Genesis 1:26-27 relate to this discussion?

4. Some skeptics argue that Jesus never claimed to be more than a prophet or reformer. They point out that most of the Gospels' overt claims to the deity of Christ come from John's gospel, the last one written, and suggest that the gospel of John is too late to be historically trustworthy. So let's read a passage from Mark's gospel, universally believed to be the earliest gospel written. Read and discuss the implications of the parable Jesus tells in Mark 12:1-12.

In the beginning was the one who is called the Word.
The Word was with God and was truly God.

— JOHN 1:1, CEV

CHAPTER FIFTEEN

God or Son of God?

I believe that the closer we get to the original Jesus the closer we are to recognizing the face of the living God.

— N. T. Wright

If we consider that in some way God came to earth through Jesus, we are faced with an infinite list of questions.

For centuries, theologians have debated the metaphysics of how Jesus can be God and yet different from God. New Testament writers emphasized his unique identity and role by referring to him as the "Son of God." However, many Christians today have not thought through its implications when they use this term.

The Bible uses the metaphor of being "God's child" to capture or describe a number of realities, all different, but all intertwined:

- On one level, all people can be thought of as God's children (see Acts 17:28). To be God's Son is to be human.
- Israel, as a whole, is said to be God's firstborn son (see Exodus 4:22-23; Hosea 11:1). To be God's Son is to be a part of Israel.
- Believers in Jesus are sometimes pictured as God's adopted children (see Romans 8:15; Galatians 4:5; Ephesians 1:5). To be God's Son is to be a member of God's family of faith.

So, when Jesus' first-century followers claimed that he was the "Son of God" (Mark 1:1, NLT; 15:39; Luke 1:35; John 1:34, TEV), what were they saying? That Jesus is human, like the rest of us? That he is Jewish? That he is a believer in God? Or something more subversive?

I think the answer is "yes" to all of the above.

God's decision to reveal himself, not just as a human being, but as a Jewish male, holds particular significance. The New Testament writers picture Jesus as the physical embodiment of the nation of Israel, which was considered collectively to be God's son. Through the events of his life, Jesus relives the story of Israel (for example, compare Hosea 11:1 with Matthew 2:15) and shows his Jewish peers how they should have interpreted and lived out Torah (one of his main topics of debate with religious leaders). God had intended that Israel would function as a light for the world, a source of hope and healing for all nations.[1] If Israel was called to shine God's light in a broad and diffuse way, Jesus was that same light in concentrated form, brought into a laser focus through one life (compare Matthew 5:14 with John 8:12; 9:5). As the perfect representative of Israel, Jesus was able to accomplish on their behalf the mission God gave to Israel.

But the leaders of the early Messiah movement were convinced that Jesus was not only a picture of a true Israelite, but of a true human, the authentic "everyman." Through Jesus, God pushed the reset button on human identity, taking us back to the garden to get a glimpse of the beautiful and loving life Adam was supposed to live in the first place (see Romans 5:12-14; 1 Corinthians 15:21-22,45-47). A movie about the life of Christ could be called *Adam Part 2: A New Beginning.*

We have never seen God, but Jesus shows us a picture of him. At the same time, we have never really seen what a perfectly functional human being looks like either, and Jesus shows us our own potential. Jesus is, in this sense, the only person ever to live a fully *human* life. This is one reason why he can be called "the way" (John 14:6) — he is the locus of communion, the point of connection between the divine and the human, between God and us (also see John 10:7-10; 1 Timothy 2:5) and he shows us in vivid clarity what we can become with God's help (see Romans 8:29).[2]

In this one human life, we see ultimate reality under a microscope. Jesus is like reality concentrate, undiluted by sin, selfishness, egoism, and religion. As we look at Jesus, study his teachings, and follow his example, we are getting to know truth in embodied form (see John 1:14; 14:6). Knowing truth, therefore, becomes a relational act rather than merely a cognitive exercise. Truth is a person to be known, not a collection of disembodied facts to be studied.

We sometimes say things like, "I've given you my heart" or "let me tell you what's in my heart." When God wants to "share his heart" with us, he gives us Jesus. This idea of God giving us his heart seems to be connected with the concept of Jesus being God's "Son"—the one he births out of himself. Consider what John, a disciple of Jesus, writes: "No one has seen God at any time; the only begotten God who is in the bosom of the Father, He has explained Him" (John 1:18, NASB).

John says that Jesus somehow comes out of God's heart (literally, bosom or chest) and into our lives. This is how God wants to communicate with us, become vulnerable with us, and show us who he really is.

As an artist "conceives" an idea, an author "labors" at her book, and a poet "gives birth" to his poem, so God's only begotten Son is God's very message of love born out of his heart and into our world.

Our family pet has a problem. We are a dog-loving family, but our dog died and we replaced it with a hamster. Snowball is a fine hamster, as far as hamsters go. But we have a lot of dog-sized love and a hamster-sized pet. This means that Snowball gets a lot of attention.[3]

It occurs to me that, although my relationship with Snowball is with *all* of him, with his fullness and fuzziness, his relationship with me is really only with my hands. When I interact with Snowball, he doesn't look me in the eyes and share a moment of tenderness. He climbs onto my hands and looks for raisins. If he thinks about the experience, I'm sure he doesn't think, "Here comes my Keeper. Ah, what a kind face he has. He looks so handsome. I like him very much." Rather, "Here come the hands. I like the hands. They give me food." Occasionally, as I hold him close to my face, he may think, "Oh, here's the nose again. I don't care for the nose. It doesn't give me anything."

My point is my hands are still me, just not *all* of me. It would be silly to think that they are something other than me. But it would be equally silly to think that they are me in my totality. I think Jesus is like God's hand, stretching down to love us in a way we can comprehend. When we speak of God's "Son" we are using symbolic language to refer to that aspect of God who became human in order to reveal God's heart.

The religious leaders who met Jesus realized the scandal involved in his claiming to be God's "Son," and they considered it blasphemy: "Now the leaders wanted to kill Jesus for two reasons. First, he had broken the law of the Sabbath. But even worse, he had said that God was his Father, which made him equal with God" (John 5:18, CEV).

To say that "Jesus is God" is true. To say he is "a part of God, yet somehow different from God" is also true. Jesus told his disciples that "the Father is greater than I" (John 14:28). In other words, what we see in finite form in Jesus is just a glimpse of the full grandeur that we call God.

By itself, the concept of this thing we call "G-o-d" is mystifying, enigmatic, and rather intimidating. But if I believe the incredible love, grace, and charity we see in Jesus gives us a glimpse of this infinite Power of the cosmos, then the universe becomes a warmer place to live.[4]

Q & Eh?

1. How would you answer someone who asked why the early Christians referred to Jesus as the "Son of God"?

2. If you have a Bible, take time to read John 1:1-18.

   - What verse or phrase stands out to you the most? Why?
   - John says in verse 3 that God created the world through the Word. How does this compare with the Genesis account

of creation? Where is "the Word" in that story (see Genesis 1:3,6,9,11,14,20,24,26; Psalm 33:6)?

- What do you think John means in verse 9?
- How does John contrast the Old Covenant (given through Moses) and the New Covenant (given through Jesus)? What are the implications of this?

3. We cannot see God, but Jesus reveals him. How can we "see" Jesus today?

No one has ever seen God. But if we love each other, God lives in us, and his love is brought to full expression in us.

— 1 JOHN 4:12, NLT

Now you are Christ's body, and individually members of it.

— 1 CORINTHIANS 12:27, NASB

CHAPTER SIXTEEN

Word of God

When Jesus revealed the new Word to the world, he did not
write a letter or a book. He simply lived it. He is the Word.
He is Word when he speaks and when he is silent,
when he is active and when he is still.

— JOHN MICHAEL TALBOT

Most religions have some form of sacred scriptures, what might be called the "Word of God."

In Jesus' day, the Jewish Scriptures were called the Torah, meaning "teaching" or "law." As we have already seen, Jesus treated the Torah as God's Word, but not God's final Word. Instead, Jesus acted like his own teaching, and even his very life was God's ultimate message to humanity. Jesus believed he was an embodied Word from God that absorbed, clarified, and "fleshed out" everything God had said before (see Matthew 5:17). What God had taught in the form of law, Jesus would now illustrate in a human life, showing how to find the principles of love embedded within the precepts of law.

The life of Jesus functions as God's illustration of everything he has been saying to humanity throughout history. It is as though God paused from teaching the world lessons and said, "Here's what I mean — watch this!" When we look at Jesus, we are seeing what all the biblical teachings should look like when lived out the way God intended.

Have you ever studied a subject or listened to a lecture that was so theoretical your mind had trouble tracking? (Perhaps that has happened during sections of this book!) At some point it all begins to sound like the schoolteacher in a Charlie Brown cartoon: Instead of hearing her words, all we hear is some variation of "Wah wah wah wah wah wah." Without illustrations, concepts can become so disembodied and theoretical that our minds have difficulty connecting them with "real" life. Worse, if the concepts we hold in our minds are never worked out in concrete form, never solidified in specific examples, we tend to redefine them as we go, usually in self-serving ways. We bend the values and principles we say we hold around our own wills as servants to our own agendas. Some examples:

"Love" (not real love, but the disembodied concept represented by the word *love*) is regularly forced into the service of human selfishness. A man can promise to love his wife until death, using "love" to refer to a lifelong commitment, a decision to pour one's life into a specific relationship. But this same man might have an affair with another woman (calling their sexual activities "making love") and then claim to "love" this new woman. In order to make sense out of his contradictory behavior, he may claim to have "fallen out of love" with his wife, the woman he originally promised to love forever, and to have "fallen in love" with someone else. He falls out of it and into it. This language of victimization helps sooth any nagging guilt ("It's not my fault—I can't help it if I fell in love"). And so he undoes the commitment of love he made to his wife in order to pursue "love" with his new interest. In other words, this man creates and recreates a fluid definition of love that serves his own egocentric agenda.

"Freedom" becomes the banner of people who choose to live selfish lives at the expense of others. They use their self-asserted "freedom" to choose a path that leads to destructive addictions, another form of imprisonment.

Similarly, religions impose rules and regulations designed to keep people on the straight and narrow. But these collections of rules and traditions don't address the real problem—our selfish hearts.[1] When law is presented as the only solution, humans soon fixate on finding ways to bend it to their own agendas, as our litigious society demonstrates.

But there is a better way.

Jesus provides skin and bones for elusive concepts like love, faith, and freedom. He shows us what they look like when fully expressed in human form. God did not just use words to reveal his truth to humankind. He knew our tendency to bend the meaning of words around our own agendas. Jesus is God's Show-and-Tell (and not just his Tell). We learn more by watching his example than any book or sermon could ever teach us. In this way, Jesus is God's "Word."

When one of Jesus' closest disciples, the apostle John, reflected on his life with Jesus, he was struck by this idea of Jesus' whole life being God's "Word" to us: "In the beginning was the Word, and the Word was with God, and the Word was God" (John 1:1). A word is a finite unit of communication. According to John, the Word of God is not just a book that God decided to write one day, but the heart of his relational essence. God's "Word" represents God's heart imparted to us (see John 1:18). It is the central message God wants us to receive: the message of his love. The Word of God is more than a book of dos and don'ts, woulds and shoulds, stories and threats designed to keep us in line. God's "Word" to humankind is God himself.

But how does he reveal himself? John goes on to explain: "The Word became flesh and made his dwelling among us. We have seen his glory, the glory of the one and only Son, who came from the Father, full of grace and truth" (John 1:14).

And the *Word* became *flesh*.

This is an amazingly revolutionary idea. When God opens his mouth to communicate his heart to humanity, a *person* comes out. His ultimate revelation of truth to humankind does not take the form of argument and assertion, page and print, chapter and verse, but personhood (see also Hebrews 1:1-2). Jesus is God's ultimate self-disclosure.

His entire life, then, is God's "Word" to us. When the Creator of the cosmos became a fetus, the Word became speechless, but no less the Word. Everything about Jesus, everything he does as well as says, is God's Word to us. Jesus is not just the Word of God become more words, but the Word of God become flesh for all to see.[2]

The Qur'an calls Christians, like Jews, "People of the Book" (see 3:64; 9:29; 29:46). Many Christians would agree with that label, but it is born out of a misunderstanding. Christ-followers are not actually people of the *Book*, but people of the *Person*. We follow Jesus, not a book that Jesus wrote. Marcus Borg explains the profound distinction:

> Indeed, one of the defining characteristics of Christianity is that we find the revelation of God primarily in *a person*, an affirmation unique among the major religions of the world. For Judaism and Islam, though Moses and Muhammad are receivers of revelation, God is not revealed in them as persons, but in the words of the Torah and Qur'an. So also in Buddhism: the Buddha as a person is not the revelation of God; rather, the Buddha's teachings disclose the path to enlightenment and compassion.
>
> But Christianity finds the primary revelation of God in a person.[3]

Follow *me*. Trust *me*. Come to *me*. *I* am the truth, says Jesus.

The implication is important. Reading, studying, and understanding the Bible is not the goal of a Christ-follower. Bible knowledge is just a first step toward the goal of following Jesus. According to Thomas Adams, "The Bible is to us what the star was to the wise men; but if we spend all our time in gazing upon it, observing its motions, and admiring its splendor, without being led to Christ by it, the use of it will be lost on us."[4]

This method of communicating himself through the person of Christ rather than through a holy book will always scandalize religious leaders. The religious "experts" (those who have dedicated their lives to the academic study of a book) may not be experts in the relationship that the Bible points toward, and others who are novices in academic study may "know" Jesus better than many religious leaders. Perhaps this is what Jesus was pointing toward when he said: "Truly I tell you, unless you change and become like children, you will never enter the kingdom of heaven" (Matthew 18:3, NRSV).

Children cannot figure out the truth through high-level academic study. But they can trust in a person as well as any educated adult. Those who want to follow the way of Jesus must decide whether they will narrowly focus only on the Bible's words as their ultimate authority or let the person of Jesus and the principles that lie behind those words be their guide.

God did not just write a book about how he works in history. God worked in history, and then people wrote a book about it.[5] Our desire should not just be to connect with God's book, but with God himself working in history. And this should include how he is working in *our* history today!

William Barclay writes:

> There was one mistake into which the early Church was never in any danger of falling. In those early days men never thought of Jesus Christ as a figure in a book. They never thought of Him as someone who had lived and died, and whose story was told and passed down in history, as the story of someone who had lived and whose life had ended. They did not think of Him as someone who had been but as someone who is. They did not think of Jesus Christ as someone whose teaching must be discussed and debated and argued about; they thought of Him as someone whose presence could be enjoyed and whose constant fellowship could be experienced. Their faith was not founded on a book; their faith was founded on a person.[6]

The Bible is like a treasure map that points the way to Jesus. But often Christians can treat the map as though it is the treasure itself, and when we do this, we miss the treasure completely.

At first this might sound like double-talk. "What do you mean by saying we should follow Jesus and not the Bible? Don't we have to read the Bible to learn about Jesus?" Of course this is true. And here is my point: If following Jesus is our goal, it will radically change how we read, interpret, and apply the Bible.

Christ-followers value the Bible, not because of its inherent value but because of its derived value. Its value comes from the treasure it points us toward. Jesus taught that this role as a pointer to Christ was the purpose of the Hebrew Scriptures, the Bible of his day, as the following two passages illustrate:

> And Jesus explained to them what was said about himself in all the Scriptures, beginning with the books of Moses and the writings of all the prophets. (Luke 24:27, TEV)

> Then he said, "When I was with you before, I told you that everything written about me in the law of Moses and the prophets and in the Psalms must be fulfilled." Then he opened their minds to understand the Scriptures. And he said, "Yes, it was written long ago that the Messiah would suffer and die and rise from the dead on the third day." (Luke 24:44-46, NLT)[7]

Jesus claims that the Bible has always pointed to him, and especially to his crucifixion as the center of his mission. The cross is the X on the treasure map. If Jesus believed that the Old Testament (that part of the Bible written before Jesus) revealed his message and mission, then this is certainly true of the New Testament (those books written explicitly about Jesus by his followers).

The Bible itself claims that before God guided his people through the Mosaic Law, the *written* Torah, he walked and talked with them in the garden, he called to them from a burning bush, he guided them as a pillar of cloud and a pillar of fire, and sometimes appeared to them incognito, in the form of a man. He made *personal* appearances.

So God's written Word is not a substitute for the Word made flesh,

Immanuel, "God with us" (Matthew 1:23). God's precepts are not a substitute for God's Spirit who continues to be God with us and within us (see John 14:16-18,26; 16:12-14; Acts 1:8; Romans 8:26-27).

Yes, religious people often confuse the treasure map with the treasure. To these people Jesus says, "You search the Scriptures because you think they give you eternal life. But the Scriptures point to me! Yet you refuse to come to me to receive this life" (John 5:39-40, NLT).

Q & Eh?

1. How is the New Testament concept of Jesus being the Word of God different from the Muslim concept of the Qur'an being God's Word? How is it similar? In what ways are Christians "People of the Book" and in what ways are they not?

2. If *Jesus* is the "Word of God," what role should the Bible play in our lives? In what ways might seeing Jesus as the Word adjust how we read the Bible?

In the beginning was the Word, and the Word was with God, and the Word was God. He was in the beginning with God. All things came into being through Him, and apart from Him nothing came into being that has come into being. In Him was life, and the life was the Light of men. . . . And the Word became flesh, and dwelt among us, and we saw His glory, glory as of the only begotten from the Father, full of grace and truth.

— JOHN 1:1-4,14, NASB

CHAPTER SEVENTEEN

Love Instead of Law

As long as a relationship is ruled by love,
the rule of law is obsolete.

— ROBERT BILMONT

It seems like almost everyone intuitively connects with the wisdom of the Golden Rule.

A few years ago, when traveling through the United States, Nina and I stayed at a bed and breakfast run by an enchanting woman. When she found out I was a pastor, she was quick to announce that she was a committed atheist. Her announcement wasn't the kind that is really saying, "I'm an atheist, so don't even try to talk to me about God, preacher man," but more along the lines of "I'm an atheist and you're a pastor—I think we could have some fun discussions." Over tea, she took the time to explain why she had rejected all religion and even God himself. She had believed in God once upon a time, but experienced a lot of relational pain in her life. When God seemed to do nothing to help her, even after she prayed earnestly, she decided that she was done with this "useless" belief. "I don't have any need for God, *and especially not for Jesus*," she emphasized. Then, with dramatic flair that suggested something mysterious would soon be revealed, she said, "I have one simple teaching that gives me all the guidance I need."

"All right. You've got me. Tell me about this teaching," I said. She took me into another room and showed me a framed statement, hanging on her wall: *Do unto others what you would have them do unto you.* "That's all you need," she said. "Follow that and you'll do well in this world." I nodded in agreement and asked her if she knew where this amazing teaching came from. She didn't, though she thought that maybe all religions say it in some way or another. I explained to her that only Jesus taught this statement the way she had it framed on her wall, as a positive call to care. This passionate atheist with "especially no need of Jesus" was quoting and orienting her life around the core teaching of Jesus. We laughed together, and acknowledged that in some way we were both committed Christ-followers, even if she didn't believe in the God Jesus talked about. One thing we both felt was true down to our bones: This teaching of Jesus is life-changing when followed, world-changing when followed by enough people: "Do for others what you want them to do for you: this is the meaning of the Law of Moses and of the teachings of the prophets" (Matthew 7:12, TEV).

In chapter 7 we talked about how Jesus shapes this universal wisdom principle into a positive call to action. Other religious teachers had taught that we should *not* do things to people that we would *not* want them to do to us. Jesus is the only one to call us to take the initiative to *do* to others what we would want them to *do* to us if we were in their shoes. This positive, other-centered orientation is love in action. Now I want to pursue this idea a little further.

My Wiccan friends have a saying that sums up their code of ethics: Harm none, and do what you want. In other words, as long as your actions are not harmful to others, then you are free to act according to your own desires, whatever they may be. This sentiment is a great first step, but it isn't exactly "loving." Love is other-centered and action-oriented. According to Jesus, it isn't good enough NOT to do bad, we must look for opportunities to actively do good! We must look for opportunities to express the practical care and loving concern to others that we would want expressed to us. This is a radical reorientation of morality for many people, religious and not. To put the emphasis of one's morality on *not* harming anyone, as many religions do, is to help people graduate to the morality of a stone. A rock doesn't hurt anyone—it just sits there, doing nothing. But we are made to love.

Last summer my daughters went to a new summer day camp that intentionally mixes campers who have mental and physical disabilities with kids with no obvious disabilities. I asked my girls to find ways each day to love others as they would want to be loved. I explained to them that it wasn't a good enough goal just not to be mean to anyone; I wanted them to find ways each day to be an encouragement to others around them. I explained that as human beings, our morality should go beyond that of a rock. So we created a Cavey Code for love: "Rock On." Each day as Nina and I dropped them off for camp, we would hold our fists high as a family and say "Rock On." At the end of the day, we would share stories of how we took the initiative, at camp or at work, to show love to others in practical ways. This is the challenge of Jesus to those who would follow him. Find ways to go beyond avoiding doing bad and to initiate love toward others. Go beyond the morality of a stone. Rock On.

I recently heard a lecture by a best-selling spiritual teacher in which he talked about how much he admired holy men in certain religions who simply do nothing as their expression of piety. They spend their days in meditation, learning to do nothing at all as their gift to humankind. They are an example of the value of being still, he said. They are to be admired for having achieved a state of true stillness, true emptiness. If only we could become like them, said this spiritual teacher. I understood what he was trying to get at, but there was no way I could agree. Sure, if suffering is an illusion and we are all just dreaming our own person-hood, then stillness is as good an approach to life as anything else. But in a world like ours, where real people hurt in many real ways, we need to do more than be stone still. We need to Rock On.

In Western culture, even those people who desire to grow in their ability to love often get bogged down in egocentric issues. For instance, Jesus said plainly, "love your neighbor as yourself" (Matthew 22:39, NRSV), but many people today use this teaching as further encour-agement to focus on the implied prerequisite of loving our neighbor:

self-love. Their thinking runs like this: "I can't love others well unless I learn to love myself, so I'd better first focus on loving myself better." And so continues the cycle of narcissism. But Jesus is not teaching that we need to learn to love ourselves better—*self-love is assumed.* If we are thirsty, we get ourselves something to drink. If we are hungry, we feed ourselves. If we are uncomfortable, we change our position. We naturally think about ourselves all the time.[1] Jesus, assuming self-love as a foundational reality, encourages us to go beyond self-centeredness to other-centeredness.

We were made for intimate friendship with God, taking shape over time as we make decisions together. Healthy friendships don't need contracts and rule lists to govern the relationship. Mutual respect and love govern well enough. As long as both people are *oriented toward* one another in other-centered love, the relationship will develop naturally without either person having to become a systems manager.

When I married Nina, we promised to love, honor, and cherish each other for the rest of our lives. Our orientation was *toward* each other, so we did not have to craft a contract with detailed rules about what that loving relationship would look like. We did not need a rule that spelled out, "If one party of the marriage is going to be late for dinner he/she must phone the other party within a reasonable amount of time." And yet, if one of us was substantially late for dinner we would know to call the other, simply because it is the *other-centered* thing to do. Our relational orientation is *toward* one another. This is very different from, say, a business contract where each party is essentially oriented *away* from the other since personal gain is usually the main motivation in such transactions. In business, you need the fine print. In marriage, the fine print will kill the relationship. Knowing the difference is crucial. When there is love, there is no need for law, for "love is the fulfillment of the law" (Romans 13:10, NASB).

Let's look at another example. If either my wife or I were to strike the other or become verbally abusive, we would hold each other accountable for these actions. We never wrote rules into our wedding vows about physical or verbal abuse, but this doesn't worry us because our relationship is love-based rather than law-based. "Love," writes N. Kenneth Rideout, "fulfills all moral and ethical responsibilities toward one another."[2]

Rule-based relationships encourage minimum morality. I drive a bit over 100 km/h on the highway that connects my home and office. Interestingly, although the speed *limit* is 100 km/h (62 mph), I still exceed it. Still, I only exceed it by what I believe I can get away with. In the back of my mind, especially when I'm rushing to an appointment that I define as important, is the question, How fast can I really go and still be ignored by the police? I have to admit that the focus of my attention is not on loving other drivers by traveling at a safe and courteous speed but the rule of the law and just how far I can bend it.[3] Law tends to cultivate a what-can-I-get-away-with mentality. This in turn encourages egocentric morality—living a certain way so we don't have to pay the fine or go to jail. Law is enough to keep a society in line, but it is not enough to change the world.

Notice that, when it comes to highway speed, the focus of my interaction with the law is how far *over* the speed limit I can reasonably get away with, not how far *under*. The fascinating truth is that humans tend to react to law by questioning how far *beyond* it they can safely go. This raises another problem with a law-based mentality. Ironically, law can cultivate increased temptation (something the apostle Paul points out in Romans 7). A law can become the moral equivalent of a childhood dare. For instance, when standing in an elevator and seeing a sign taped to the wall that reads, "Wet Paint: Do Not Touch," what do you immediately want to do? Exactly.

Yes, we need law to govern our societies because people do not automatically love as they should. But in truly loving relationships, whether that is a marriage, a friendship, or our relationship with God, law is always second best.

Throughout the Bible, God likens the relationship he desires to have with his people to a marriage. This makes sense since marriage is the ultimate human relationship where love fully replaces law.

When *entering* a marriage our orientation should be *toward* our partner, and so we need only promise to love and then spend the rest of our lives working out what that loving relationship will look like. Note that this love is based on promise, on choice, on commitment, on covenant; not on emotion. In the day-to-day rhythms of this relationship, one partner expresses his or her desires (not rules) and the other responds eagerly because of the other-centered love they share. My wife, for instance, holds all her stress in her shoulders so she often asks me to give her a massage. I do, not because we have made a rule that *makes* me do this, but because I *want* to respond positively to her needs and desires. This is how a love relationship between adults works—other-centered attention responding to desires and needs, with no rules in sight.

Now, when *exiting* a marriage, everything changes. When a divorce occurs, people's orientation is *away from* their partner, so the details of law take center stage. Law and love are two entirely different ways of being, analogous to the difference between marriage vows and separation agreements.

Jesus taught that all God wants for his relationship with us is what any marriage should be—a loving, other-centered, law-free relationship. Certainly our relationship with God may be more than any human marriage, but it definitely should not be less.

Q & Eh?

1. Let's brainstorm. This chapter gives a few examples of the problems that can arise when we function in law mode rather than love mode. What are some other examples from different situations in your life where functioning according to law creates problems? School? Work? Family?

2. What are some of the risks of calling people to live by love instead of law? Can you think of examples? Do you think it is worth the risk?

3. Some forms of religion make a mental state of enlightenment their chief aim. Devotees can spend a large percentage of their time on earth trying to perfect a specific state of conscious awareness through meditation, stillness, and various forms of deprivation. What might be some of the positive effects of this form of religious practice? What could be the downside of this kind of religious pursuit?

4. In Matthew 12:1-8, Jesus offers the religious leaders of his day some examples from their own Scriptures of God's delighting in his people's prioritizing love over law. Then, in the following verses (Matthew 12:9-14) he provides his own example. If/when you have a Bible handy, read the passage. What verse stands out to you the most? Why? What is so subversive about Jesus' statements in verses 6 and 8? Why do you think the religious leaders resisted Jesus' teaching?

—◆◆◇◆◆—

I want you to show love,
not offer sacrifices.
I want you to know me
more than I want burnt offerings.

— HOSEA 6:6, NLT

—◆◆◇◆◆—

CHAPTER EIGHTEEN

Back to the Garden

We are stardust, we are golden, and we've got to get ourselves back to the garden.

— JONI MITCHELL

The world's best-selling book, a book most people think is about religion, begins by establishing what should have been a world *without* religion. The opening chapters of the Bible describe a religionless world as God's original design. Religion was not a part of life in the garden, and God did not design us for it.

From a biblical point of view, religion is a later development, and one that had mixed results. At best, the way of rules and rituals gives people who are not yet sensitized to God's relational presence some extra help (see Matthew 19:8). At worst, the way of rules and rituals intrudes into people's spiritual lives and distracts from, more than it leads to, relationship with God (see Romans 7:4-11; 2 Corinthians 3:5-7).

Regardless of whether or not we take the story of Adam and Eve as history or metaphor, the absence of religious rituals and routines in their story is key to understanding the rest of the Bible.[1] In the beginning, we are told, God created human beings for intimate relationship with himself and with each other (see Genesis 2:18-25). Together, people and God lived in deep connection, cocreating new life (see Genesis 1:26-27) and tending creation (see Genesis 2:15).

God spoke: "Let us make human beings in our image, make them
         reflecting our nature
So they can be responsible for the fish in the sea,
         the birds in the air, the cattle,
And, yes, Earth itself,
         and every animal that moves on the face of Earth."
God created human beings;
         he created them godlike,
Reflecting God's nature.
         He created them male and female.
God blessed them:
         "Prosper! Reproduce! Fill Earth! Take charge!
Be responsible for fish in the sea and birds in the air,
         for every living thing that moves on the face of Earth."
                  (Genesis 1:26-28, MSG)

God could have made a world that was self-sustaining, in which
we passively spent our days as consumers instead of contributors. But a
world like that is not a fit for beings who are created to reflect the divine
image. We are by nature creative beings, made in the image and likeness
of the Creator. We were made to exercise our Godlike creativity on earth
as his representatives, tenderly caring for all creation. It was therefore
natural for God to manifest his presence to Adam and Eve in humanlike
ways, since humankind reflects his own image and likeness (see Genesis
1:26; 3:8). In Eden we see God and people, Creator and creation, walking and talking together in the cool of the evening breeze, living life in
intimate partnership. This is the life God intended for us.

For too long, people have assumed that *religion* is how we connect
with God, whereas *relationship* is how we connect with people. The original lesson of the Bible is that our connection with God should be a lot
more like our relationships with other persons—intimate, unscripted,
authentic.

Rituals and routines, institutions and organizations, may be used by people as meaningful expressions of genuine faith, but they are not to be confused with the substance of that faith. The Old Testament prophets repeatedly called Israel "back to the garden"—back to "walking with God" relationally, passionately, actively. God wasn't against symbolic gestures and rituals; he wanted these gestures to be infused with real meaning supported by lives of mercy, justice, passion, and love. God is like a lover who doesn't just want to receive flowers, but flowers that are accompanied by an attitude of true love and service.

> With what shall I come before the LORD
>   and bow down before the exalted God?
> Shall I come before him with burnt offerings,
>   with calves a year old?
> Will the LORD be pleased with thousands of rams,
>   with ten thousand rivers of olive oil?
> Shall I offer my firstborn for my transgression,
>   the fruit of my body for the sin of my soul?
> He has shown all you people what is good.
>   And what does the LORD require of you?
> To act justly and to love mercy
>   and to walk humbly with your God. (Micah 6:6-8)

Walking with God. Doing life together. Consciously being with God in the moment-by-moment experiences of our lives. This is faith—the trust that is the foundation for any purposeful partnership. By placing Adam and Eve in a "garden" (Genesis 2:8,15), God was calling all humankind to partner with him in caring for creation.

A garden is a meeting place between nature and human culture. It reflects both divine and human creativity, as opposed to the extremes of a city on the one hand and a forest (or jungle, depending on how tropical you like your analogies) on the other. Genesis shows us that God's original design for humanity was an intimate, purposeful relationship between himself and humanity, expressed through a cocreative partnership. Like John Lennon, God imagined a place with no religion. He called it Eden and spoke it into existence.

If it is true that a world without religion was God's original design, then it is also true that a world without religion is God's final goal for us. From a biblical perspective, salvation is not ultimately about going to heaven as a disembodied spirit, but about the renewal of all creation back to what it should have been in the first place (see Isaiah 11:1-9; 55; Romans 8:18-25; 2 Peter 3:13). Just as Adam and Eve walked and talked directly with God in the garden with no intermediating religious institution getting in the way, so the Bible says that God's desire for us is to come back to experiencing a face-to-face intimacy with himself (see 1 Corinthians 13:12).

In the book of Revelation, chapters 21 and 22, the final state of humankind is described, and it isn't what we might expect. No clouds, no harps, no cream cheese. Instead, the Bible says we are on a return journey to the world, this world, as God originally intended it to be. The author makes the point by highlighting the fact that there is no temple in this brave new world (see Revelation 21:22). As we've already discussed, the temple was *the* institution that connected people with God in first-century Israel, the focus of the rituals of sacrifice and cleansing. But in this final state, says the book of Revelation, God himself will act as the temple. No more forms, no more structures, no more rituals to connect us with God. The story of the Bible, then, is the story of the many detours and sidetracks taken by humanity on its way back to intimate union with God, and the many ways God helps us along the way. Ultimately it is the story of God not just *revealing* a pathway, but *becoming* the pathway back to the garden. This is the meaning of Jesus. One day he will bring it about for all of creation, but in the meantime, we can begin to experience this intimacy *now*.

So when Jesus arrives on the scene, he points people back to the garden, regularly reminding religious leaders of the way the world was originally meant to be (see Matthew 19:1-9). Jesus says that God is calling us back to our original state of intimate and creative relationship with himself and with each other *directly,* minus the need for the mediating traditions of religion.

Jesus goes so far as to say that even the law God gave Israel for a period of time (recorded in what Christians call the "Old Testament") was God's *compromise* with humanity because of what he calls our "hardness of heart" (Matthew 19:8, NASB).[2] In other words, people had become too self-centered, too ego-driven, too relationally stunted to live in healthy relationships with God and each other apart from the explicit direction of rules, rituals, and routines. So rule-based living may have had a role to play for a time, but now that time is passed.

Q & Eн?

1. Rather than put Adam and Eve in a city or a jungle, God chose to put them in a garden, a place of partnership between divine and human creativity. I have heard it said that every time God decides he wants to do something in history, his very next thought is, "Now, with whom can I do it?" He is all about relationship. Think of Bible stories involving Abraham, Moses, Joshua, and Jesus. (If you are not familiar enough with the Bible, just skip this question.)

   - How does God show his desire for partnership with people in each of these stories?
   - Can you think of other biblical examples of God partnering with people?
   - In what ways might God want to partner with you to accomplish great things?

2. We were left in charge of the planet — and look at the mess we've made. Why do you think many religious people tend not to put their energies into caring for creation?

3. Jesus said that the Old Testament laws were necessary because of our "hardness of heart." He also went on to undo, challenge, and nullify those very rules. What hopeful thing is Jesus implying about the human heart?

———◆◆◆———

I did not see a temple there.
The Lord God All-Powerful and the Lamb were its temple.

— REVELATION 21:22, CEV

———◆◆◆———

CHAPTER NINETEEN

It's Time to Grow Up

God has acted to set the world right and to rescue us from slavery
to human religious programs.

— RICHARD B. HAYS

Doesn't the Bible teach that God himself originated at least the Hebrew religion? Didn't he make a personal appearance on Mount Sinai to deliver the Law to Moses? Doesn't this body of Law (called the Torah or Teaching) go way beyond the Ten Commandments to include hundreds of religious rules, rituals, and routines? If God calls us to abandon religion, why would he have introduced his people to some form of it in the first place? If God changed his modus operandi with humankind through Jesus, does that mean he had made a mistake that needed to be undone? Was Jesus sent to tell us that God changed his mind about religion?

There are many scenarios where developing circumstances call for a developmental approach. In these situations, the need for change does not nullify the fact that the original approach was appropriate for its time. We treat a seed differently once it becomes a plant, even though it has not essentially changed in substance. In the same way, Jesus treats the Old Testament as the seed that gives birth to something wonderfully new: "Jesus asked, 'What is the Kingdom of God like? What shall I compare it with? It is like this. A man takes a mustard seed and plants it in his field. The plant grows and becomes a tree, and the birds make their nests in its branches" (Luke 13:18-19, TEV).

From seed to plant to tree to home for other living things. Same substance, different stages; each stage right for its time, but eventually needing to give way to something greater.

No matter how much Jesus tries to call his fellow Israelites into a different way of interpreting and applying Torah, he never says that Torah itself was a mistake. He does, however, tell us that we need a new understanding and application of it (see Matthew 5:17-48; 12:1-8). His earliest followers make the same case in their writings (see Romans and Galatians)—the Law is still good, but its role in our lives must change.

Parents know that different stages of child development require different parenting styles. This evolving method does not nullify the validity of earlier styles. Rather, it simply means that each style is appropriate to the developmental level of the child. Throughout the Bible God uses the analogy of parenthood to teach us about our relationship with him. As God's children, we can expect him to parent us appropriately through our various stages of spiritual growth. When young, children need stricter rules and tighter boundaries. As we grow up, the rules can relax, and we can get to know our parents, not only as parents, but also as friends. When we are young, we need to be told what to do, what to wear, how to behave, what to eat. As children grow older, every parent hopes that the instructions received in childhood will become internalized *principles* of adult living.

I have two daughters (and, as I write this, one more on the way!). When Chelsea and Chanelle were younger, my wife and I would have to tell them what to wear when going out, how much of their meal they had to finish, when they had to go to bed, where they could ride their scooters, what they could watch on television, and so on. I didn't mind that. It is part of parenting. But it is only an early stage of parenting. If, however, after a number of years my girls are still calling me from university and asking "Daddy, what can I wear today?" or "Do I have to finish all my vegetables?" or "What time do I have to go to bed tonight?" I am not going to consider myself a successful parent. Successful parenting is a process of early instruction leading to later internalization and incorporation. What start out as rules and routines should eventually become principles and priorities that our children carry with them into their adult lives.

The very same is true for God and his kids. In the earlier stages of humanity, our spiritual dad gave us the same kind of rules, regulations, and routines that all children need. However, that phase of a parent-child relationship can never be an end in itself, but a means to an end. Old Covenant Law was valuable as a tutor (see Galatians 3:24-25), and still is valuable as a source of divine principles (see Matthew 5:17-18). However, God's goal for humanity has always been to move us toward personal relationship with him as friends (see John 15:15).

This is why Christ-followers should value the Old Testament as Scripture, truth teaching, without the obligation to practice every dietary law or religious routine. Although the principles are timeless, the specific practice of those principles may now be obsolete (see Hebrews 8: 6-13). Behind every rule parents give their children is a lasting principle; it should be the principles, not the rules, that endure.

This is a recurring theme in the New Testament. The apostle Paul went so far as to compare young children with slaves on one specific point—both are forced to follow rules, whether or not they understand or agree with them. His point, when writing to the early Christian community, was that Jesus came to help us move out of that "slavery" to religious rules and into a new spiritual freedom:

> I want to tell you this: While those who will inherit their fathers' property are still children, they are no different from slaves. It does not matter that the children own everything. While they are children, they must obey those who are chosen to care for them. But when the children reach the age set by their fathers, they are free. It is the same for us. We were once like children, slaves to the useless rules of this world. But when the right time came, God sent his Son who was born of a woman and lived

204 THE END OF RELIGION

under the law. God did this so he could buy freedom for those who were under the law and so we could become his children. (Galatians 4:1-5, NCV)

"Useless rules of this world"—that is what religion amounts to when we focus on the precepts instead of the principles. God has a message for religious people who still cling to these useless rules: *It's time to grow up.*

Just before the death of actor W. C. Fields, a friend visited Fields' hospital room and was surprised to find him thumbing through a Bible. Asked what he was doing with a Bible, Fields replied, "I'm looking for loopholes." And that is another problem with rule-based living—we can too easily develop a loophole mentality.

When I was a child, I was a legalist with a strong will. Rules were the language I understood, and I tried to bend them to my advantage. Once, when one of my older sisters was trying to do her homework at the dining room table, I took it upon myself to bug her. Why? I don't know. I just felt it was my civic duty as the younger brother to pester my sister from time to time, and I had determined that this was going to be one of those important duty-fulfilling moments.

My dad intervened by reminding me, "It's reading time for you, young man—all right?" I knew what he meant. After school I had to read a chapter from whatever book I was currently reading through, giving my sister some quiet space to do her homework. But I had already embarked on my mission to pester my older sister, so I listened to my father's words but not his meaning. When he returned, he found me still hovering around my sister, pestering her in a variety of ways. When he reminded me that we had agreed it was reading time, I said, "You said it was reading time, but you didn't say *I* have to read."

My dad is a patient man, so he simply turned up the dial on the detail of his instruction. "By telling you it is reading time, I mean that *you* have to read—all right?" I heard his words but again ignored his meaning. When he left I continued hovering around my sister, reading aloud pages out of my sister's book and other printed material I could find, bugging her to no end. When my dad returned he was obviously losing his patience, but my "spidey sense" told me I could get away with pushing things a bit further. "What is going on here?" he asked. I replied, "You told me I have to read, but you didn't tell me *what* I have to read."

My father obviously knew that I was in game-playing mode, and he clamped down on the situation with increased detail and authority. "Here's what you have to do, son. You have to read your own book, while sitting on the couch in the living room, and you may not get off the couch or stop reading until I tell you. Understood?" I agreed. It was easy to agree—I already knew the loophole he had left open for me. I grabbed my reading book, sat on the couch in the living room, and began reading my book—out loud—very loud—bug-my-sister-who-is-trying-to-do-her-homework-in-the-next-room loud—each word enunciated with irritating phonetic precision. There was something satisfying about having the ability to "beat the system" up to this point. Eventually, my dad beat my system, and I had to submit to some thorough rules, including sitting on the couch, reading my own book *silently*, and not making any sounds, including dramatic page turning or heavy sighs, until he released me from the task.

My dad never missed an opportunity to teach his kids an important lesson, and after my reading time was finally over, he used my legalistic attitude as an illustration of the teaching of Jesus. He said, "You know I love you very much. And that means that I always want what's best for you. I believe you love me too, and your sister, but that means you should want what is best for us too. You should want your sister to do well in school, and you should want to listen to me when I ask you to do something. You knew what I meant when I first told you it was reading time, and your love should have motivated you to obey what I meant. You know I finally got you to do the right thing—to read to yourself and stop bugging your sister. But I had to use a lot of rules to get you to do the right thing. I had to parent you with law to get you to act out your love. You fought against love. You made the rules necessary because you weren't ready to love. I know you are young, but I want you to know that I don't like the way you were today. I want you to learn how to love, not just force you to obey the rules. I guess what I'm saying is, *it's time to grow up.*"

If you try to follow the Bible's teaching like a rule book, you are functioning on a spiritually immature level. Jesus challenged the Pharisees on this point over and over again (see Matthew 12:1-8).[1] Rules become necessary where love does not lead our behavior. Today, I try to pass on to my kids the same gift my father gave me. I tell my girls that I don't want them to just follow the rules, but the reason behind the rules. Thanks, Dad.

Q & Eʜ?

1. Some Bible-believing churches have an oft-repeated motto: "The Bible says it. That settles it. I believe it. Let's do it." What could be some problems inherent with this kind of attitude? How would you rewrite this motto to better reflect the teachings of Jesus?

2. Money is one area of our lives where we often look for loopholes: taxes, duty, profits, charity. Jesus often rebukes religious people for being immature and irresponsible with wealth. Read Luke 12:13-34 and 16:13-15.

   • How do you think religious institutions might mishandle money today?
   • In what ways do *you* likewise mishandle money?
   • In light of Jesus' teaching that our hearts will always bend toward what we invest our money in (see Luke 12:34), what practical steps could you take in your own life to invest your money and possessions in what is most important?

3. Are there any ethical areas in your life where you are currently investing your energy looking for loopholes rather than following the high standard of love?

———◆◆✕◆◆———

When I was a child, I spoke like a child, I thought like a child,
I reasoned like a child; when I became an adult,
I put an end to childish ways.

— 1 CORINTHIANS 13:11, NRSV

———◆◆✕◆◆———

CHAPTER TWENTY

Religion Versus Relationship

Religion is the archrival of intimate spirituality. . . . Religion,
a tiresome system of manmade dos and don'ts, woulds and
shoulds — impotent to change human lives but tragically
capable of devastating them — is what is left after a true
love for God has drained away. Religion is the shell that
is left after the real thing has disappeared.

— DOUG BANISTER

Jesus pointed people toward a spirituality that was and is subversively simple. He never used the word "religion" to describe what he envisioned for his followers. Instead, he said he wanted people simply to "know" God (John 17:3). In Bible times, "knowing" someone was a common euphemism for sex (for example, Matthew 1:25, KJV, says that Mary was a virgin because Joseph "did not know her till she had brought forth her first born Son"). Knowing someone, whether sexually or not, usually referred to having an intimate union with them. Jesus emphasized this union with God through one of his favorite words — *faith* (see Matthew 9:29; 17:20; Mark 1:15; 5:36; 11:22; Luke 7:50; 18:8; John 3:14-18; 6:29; 7:38; 8:24; 11:25-26; 12:36,44-46; 14:1; 17:20-21).[1]

I heard the story of a child who was asked in Sunday school to define *faith*. His answer? "Faith is when you believe in something that you know isn't true." Well, at least he had the chutzpah to say what many of us think. But this definition is based on a misunderstanding about the nature of faith.

Faith is a deeply relational concept. It means "trust" or "trustworthiness." Both the Hebrew *emunah* (used in the Old Testament) and the Greek *pistis* (used in the New Testament) have the double meaning of faith and faithfulness, trust and trustworthiness. *Faith is the belief or trust in a person that moves us to act lovingly and loyally toward that person.* It is not believing something that runs against our intellect, but moving beyond intellect to experience. If I have faith in Jesus, this means that I trust him enough to follow him, to embrace his teachings for my life. Dallas Willard states it simply, "Remember, to believe something is to act as if it is so."[2]

I love my wife. I trust her. I have faith in her. And I am faithful to her. This faith is not unreasonable or anti-intellectual, but neither is it merely an academic process. It is *relational*, which is a higher way of knowing. So faith and reason are not opposites (as people sometimes set them up to be), but just different categories of knowing. I *know* 2 + 2 = 4. I also *know* my wife. One is reason; the other is relationship. The faith I have in Nina is not unreasonable or contrary to evidence—it just goes far beyond reason to intimacy.

According to Jesus' use of the word, to have "faith" is not so much to believe a certain checklist of theology or to participate in a specific list of rituals, but to trust in a Person, to be committed to that Person, to be *oriented toward* rather than *away from* that Person.

The Christian religion tends to codify the teaching of Jesus and then mandates that adherents place their faith in the resulting "orthodox" doctrine. To question any doctrine is to question Christ. But Jesus calls us to place our faith in *him*. Marcus Borg helps us distinguish the difference:

> To believe *in* a person is quite different from believing *that* a series of statements about the person are true. . . . *Believing that* and *believing in* are very different. The first leads to an emphasis

on correct belief, on believing the right things. The second leads to a transformed life.[3]

On one occasion, some spiritual seekers came to Jesus to ask him what "work" God would require them to do. No doubt their religious background prepared them to receive a response that included a variety of detailed duties: pray this much, read that much, give this much, take that pilgrimage, do these things, avoid those things, and so on. His advice, however, was almost too simple for them to grasp: "The work of God is this: to believe in the one he has sent" (John 6:28-29).

Trust me, says Jesus. Get to *know* me. These people expected rules. He offered relationship.

Representing God to us, Jesus says "Follow *me*" (Matthew 4:19; 9:9; John 1:43; 10:27; 21:19,22; emphasis added). He does not say follow this new religion I am starting.

So what happened? What went so terribly wrong? How did the Christian *religion* get started? It is as though Jesus said, "Here is the good news: Religion is REDUNDANT! You no longer need any system of rules, rituals, and routines to approach God! He has come to you to offer divine love, forgiveness, and blessing directly!" And then, over the next few centuries, his followers said, "What a fantastic idea! We should build a religion out of that! We'll call it the Christian religion, and we'll have our own set of rules, rituals, and routines that people have to follow, all in the name of Jesus."

The Christian *faith* is the phenomenon of people following Jesus. The Christian *religion* is the phenomenon of people following the phenomenon of people following Jesus. The Christian religion puts the emphasis on the institution and the traditions it stewards, rather than the person of Jesus. I imagine the difference looking something like this:

CHRISTIAN FAITH (X)
The Phenomenon of People Following Jesus

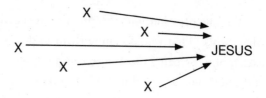

CHRISTIAN RELIGION (Y)
The Phenomenon of People Following
The Phenomenon of People Following Jesus

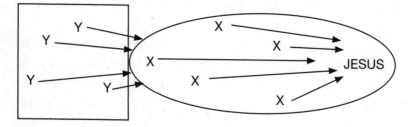

When faith becomes religion, people on the inside of the group begin to focus their attention on the perimeter, patrolling the boundaries to regulate who is in and who is out. They develop visible boundary markers, demarcations of holiness, which become important signs of group identity. As we saw in part 2, Jesus challenged this specific phenomenon in the religion of his day. The question is (and here I am addressing people who claim to follow Jesus): Are we willing to pick up that challenge today and to keep our eyes fixed on Jesus as the only source and goal of our faith (see Hebrews 12:2) rather than on the multiple lines of religious demarcation that define our group identity? In other words, are we willing to focus on our center instead of our perimeter?

As Gregory Boyd points out in his book *Repenting of Religion*, groups that focus on their center may have less clear perimeters. But they will not be threatened by this *perimeter ambiguity*, because they are clear about the core of their identity. This, in turn, leads to greater compassion and acceptance.[4] Without having to believe utopian ideas like "all people go to heaven when they die" or "sin is illusion" or "all religions are equally valid," Jesus-followers will not try to separate who is "saved" and who is not, who is in and who is out. Policing the perimeter is what religious people do, but not Christ-followers—at least, not Christ-followers who really want to follow Christ.

To borrow an image from Jesus, his followers will allow wheat and weeds to grow alongside each other because they know *they* aren't supposed to do the judging/separating (see Matthew 13:24-30). Jesus promoted a nonjudgmental spirituality. He did not say there would be no judgment from God at the end of our lives, but that in the present his followers should not try to do this work on God's behalf (see John 3:17; 12:47-48). Those who follow Jesus are called to represent God's *love* to others, but not his judgment (see Romans 12:19-21).

It took Jesus' disciples a while to replace their religious, border-patrolling mentality with a more embracing faith. When they heard of other people acting like they were Christ-followers but without showing all of the signs the disciples wanted to see, they complained to Jesus, hoping he would support their efforts to oppose these borderline believers. Christ's response illustrates his belief that peripheral issues must not define his movement—"Whoever is not against us is with us" (Mark 9:41, NCV).[5]

When sinful, broken, hurting people are pleasantly surprised at how accepting we are, and religious people are outraged at how accepting we are, there is a good chance we're starting to live like Jesus. We will have finally learned the difference between *acceptance* and *agreement*—a lesson religious people find hard to grasp.

I once had a long conversation with my Jehovah's Witness friends about the beauty of following Jesus rather than following an institution that claims to be following Jesus, such as the Watchtower Bible and Tract Society, the organization that receives their utmost loyalty. We used to meet weekly to study the Bible together—I thought I was converting them and they thought they were converting me. Everyone was happy. We talked about doctrinal differences and conflicting Bible interpretations, but a light went on for me when I realized that our center, our focus, was not the same. We were not two kinds of Jesus-followers trying to figure out how best to live out his teachings. My friends were more uncritically loyal to an organization than to Jesus. They believed that only through membership in the Watchtower Bible and Tract Society ("God's organization on earth," as they called it) could someone truly come to know God, because only this organization teaches completely true doctrine about God. Oh sure, they could admit to the organization's making mistakes in its teaching from time to time, such as making clear predictions about the date of Christ's return which never came true. But they still believed that their trust must be placed in Watchtower doctrine and they must be baptized by a Jehovah's Witness leader if they were to truly please God.

I turned to John 17:3, where Jesus says in a prayer to the Father, "Eternal life is to *know* you, the only true God, and to *know* Jesus Christ, the one you sent" (CEV, emphasis added). To "know" God, I contended, is a relational act and not just educational. Sure, knowing someone may involve learning accurate information about him, but it happens through direct engagement, not through academic study.

Interestingly, Jehovah's Witnesses have their own Bible translation (the *New World Translation of the Holy Scriptures*) that slightly adjusts the text of John 17:3 to say, "This means everlasting life, their taking in knowledge of you, the only true God, and of the one whom you sent forth, Jesus Christ." Do you see the subtle change that changes everything? Simply "knowing" God has become "taking in knowledge of" God. For them, finding accurate information about God shrewdly replaces a relational connection with God. And, of course, this doctrine is accompanied by the teaching that only the Watchtower Bible and

Tract Society has that right information that we need. And with that, a theological system of dependence on the organization for salvation has been created. Salvation through the system, offered door-to-door.

I challenged my Jehovah's Witness friends that their organizational dependence for salvation misses the point of the good news of Jesus. I told them that by making the Watchtower Bible and Tract Society a necessary mediator of truth between God and us, they were effectively rewriting 1 Timothy 2:5 to read, "For there is one God and one mediator between God and people—and that mediator is the Watchtower Bible and Tract Society" (as opposed to Jesus, as the text actually says).

When we follow Jesus, we spend our lives working out that relationship in grace-filled ways, and we celebrate the diversity of others who want to follow Jesus as well. But when we replace our fidelity to Jesus with loyalty to an institution or organization, we then see people outside our specific organization as the competition rather than as extended spiritual family. Sadly, I see this mentality festering in many Christian denominations today.

There are many people who bear the name "Christian" who have joined a group and taken a label, but have not entered into a trust-based relationship with the person of Jesus. They just don't *know* him. And I suppose there are many people who love and follow Jesus who may not fit neatly into many of the groups, churches, and denominations that bear the title "Christian." On Judgment Day there may be plenty of surprises:

> "Not everyone who says to me, 'Lord, Lord,' will enter the kingdom of heaven, but only those who do the will of my Father who is in heaven. Many will say to me on that day 'Lord, Lord, did we not prophesy in your name and in your name perform many miracles?' Then I will tell them plainly, '*I never knew you.* Away from me, you evildoers!'" (Matthew 7:21-23, emphasis added)

Q & Eh?

1. How is knowing someone or something by faith different from knowing by reason? Why is this significant?

2. What are some differences between the Christian *faith* and the Christian *religion*?

3. If no organization is the one way to God, does this mean that we should never belong to an organization as part of our spiritual expression? Or do organizations, churches, denominations, and other forms of spiritual groups have a positive role to play in our lives?

4. The apostle Paul writes, "There is one God and one mediator between God and human beings, Christ Jesus, himself human" (1 Timothy 2:5).

   • What about this statement would be considered subversive in his day?
   • What are the implications of this teaching for our day?

5. Which graphic on the following page do you think best represents the teaching of Jesus about salvation, where "X" is a true Christ-follower and "Y" is someone who is not, and the circle represents the recognized borders of "orthodox" Christian religion? Why?

Theory A: Boundary Markers Define Identity

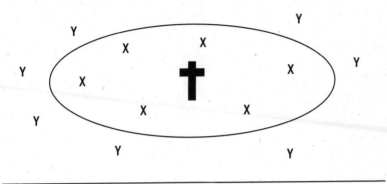

Theory B: Heart, Attitude, and Orientation Define Identity

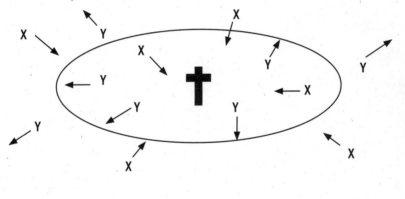

"Whoever is not against us is with us."

— MARK 9:41, NCV

CHAPTER TWENTY-ONE

So What?

Religion, therefore, is a loser, a strictly fallen activity. It has a
failed past and a bankrupt future. There was no religion in Eden
and there won't be any in heaven; and in the meantime Jesus has
died and risen to persuade us to knock it all off right now.

— ROBERT FARRAR CAPON

If you have made it this far and have tracked with me through this book, you may be ready to conclude, as many have, that this world would be a far better place without religion—and I believe you would be right—sort of. Although true, this conclusion is incomplete. With nothing to fill the void, the result of doing away with religion would hardly be an improvement. History bears this out. For every violent religious fundamentalist there is a violent secular fundamentalist. For every Osama bin Laden there is a Stalin.

Nature abhors a vacuum, and so does the human heart. The human soul was created for a purpose. To be fully authentic, to become what it was made to be, the human soul needs more than the absence of something; it needs the presence of Someone. We were designed to live within the context of a relationship with Divine Consciousness, the Personhood of God.

This concept of intimate and interactive relationship with God, a relationship of naked intimacy, delight, and passion, was at the core of Jesus' teaching and abundantly evident in his own life. Experiencing God as Father, Mother, Husband, Lover, Friend, Counselor, and Guide is the teleological center in Jesus' teaching—the goal he is leading us toward.

The beautiful thing about relating to God is that we don't need to master any one technique or tool to do so. I have spoken to people who have disciplined themselves in multiple religious techniques and practiced them regularly for years with the hope of one day being enlightened. While their dedication is commendable, I believe they have missed something wonderful about God. Our "enlightenment" can come in a moment, once we realize that God is a person who loves us and desires intimate relationship with us. When that reality fully seizes us, a light goes on that can never be put out. We *are* enlightened. Then the rest of our lives can be spent enjoying and deepening that relationship through a variety of means.

Notice the difference. Christ-followers participate in spiritual practices (like prayer, Bible study, and meditation), not in order to *achieve* something, but in order to better *experience* what they already know to be true. I talk with my wife, not in order to *achieve* marriage, but in order to *experience* the marriage we have. In many religions, the techniques of prayer and/or meditation and/or reading sacred Scripture are used to somehow achieve illumination or connection with the divine. But according to Jesus, the connection already exists, as far as God is concerned. All we have to do is welcome it. God's loving presence surrounds us like air; it is the atmosphere we live in (see Acts 17:28)—we simply need to stop holding our breath.

Once we have accepted God's love as a fact of life, the inescapable atmosphere of our lives, we are free to participate in activities like prayer, church attendance, and Scripture study as expressions of the life God gives us, but not as techniques to obtain that life.

When Jesus talks about spiritual practices like prayer, giving to charity, and fasting, he never prescribes any one religious routine to follow. Instead he gives guidelines to keep these practices focused on relationship with God rather than on appearance. He assumes that once we have a right view of God and a right desire to connect with

God, then we'll pray and dialogue with God because we want to, not because our religion mandates it. So he begins his teaching on prayer by saying "*When* you pray" (see Matthew 6:5-7), assuming we will pray, rather than "You *must* pray, and you must pray this many times a day, in this manner, facing in this direction," etc. For Jesus, prayer is assumed rather than commanded because he sees prayer as a relational act between two loving parties who *want* to communicate.

Jesus speaks of the "new wine" of his message needing "fresh wineskins" (Matthew 9:17, NASB) — those structures, patterns, and ways of living that contain and transport the substance. As new wine ferments and expands, the wineskin that contains it must likewise stretch along with it. If we try to put new wine in an old wineskin that has become brittle and cannot stretch any more, it will eventually burst open and the wine will be lost.

Jesus is not against the wineskin of structure. All relationships can benefit from a degree of flexible structure, and our relationship with God is no different in this way. But Jesus emphasizes that *structure must submit to substance, the forms of religion must be molded by the essence of faith, and not the other way around.* Patterns of spiritual exercise must remain flexible and relational, lest we try to contain the new wine within antiquated and inflexible traditions that simply cannot contain the fullness of the ever-expanding wine of the gospel. Wineskins are needed, but only as vehicles for the wine. And no one wineskin is sacrosanct.

If you are a religious person, ask yourself this: What would happen if your religious institution or denomination were to close down entirely? What difference would that make to God's activity on the planet? If your church, denomination, or long-standing tradition ended, would God's way of salvation be hindered? If you think your religious tradition or organization is indispensable to God's saving activity on planet Earth, then you are clinging to a brittle wineskin. I once spoke with a religious leader who claimed that his church tradition could be traced back to Jesus and was the true "wineskin" that held Christ's new wine for all to access. Obviously, we had to agree to disagree. I believe he missed the point of the good news Jesus brought, that no one wineskin is the way to God.

Once the wineskin of a particular structure, tradition, or organization becomes our focus, the benefit of the wine will be missed. *No one ever quenched their thirst by chewing on a wineskin.*

The question for all of us who have a religious background is this: Can we say along with the apostle Paul that we consider our religious heritage "crap" when compared to the spiritual intimacy of knowing Jesus by faith? This is his sentiment expressed in Philippians 3:2-9, where Paul uses the Greek word *skubalon*, meaning "dung" or "excrement" to describe the importance of his religious wineskin when compared to the wine itself.[1]

Do I believe this about the church and denomination that I am a part of? Absolutely. Because I am a pastor of a church that seems healthy and vibrant, occasionally someone asks me about the question of sustainability: "What are the leaders of The Meeting House doing to ensure that the organization endures in good form for the next generation?" Although there are some specific things I could mention in response, my answer always begins with this question: What makes you think we think The Meeting House needs to endure?[2] Organizational expressions of faith and spirituality can come and go. These forms are shadows, expressions of the reality of faith itself. When we embrace the fact that no one church or institution or organization or denomination *must* endure, we can begin to free ourselves of the bondage of systems maintenance. Knowing that no organization is indispensable to God, I can celebrate the *present* health of The Meeting House and delight in how God is using this organization for now without worrying about the future. This is joyfully freeing, and deeply restful.[3]

So here is the great irony — Jesus is happy to see his followers get organized in order to help spread the message that organizations are not the answer. Christ-followers read the Bible to learn of Jesus' teaching that reading the Bible is not what makes us a Christian. We pray regularly in order to commune with the God who reminds us that praying regularly is not what makes us acceptable to him. We meditate to immerse our souls in the love of God that is already ours, not in order to somehow achieve a state of self-induced enlightenment. And we go to church to collectively celebrate the message that going to church is not what makes us God's children.

A Christ-follower acknowledges that going to church doesn't make you a Christian any more than walking in the woods makes you a tree. And once that is understood and embraced, a church community can become more of a "come as you are" party than a religious obligation, a celebration of the life we're given, not a religious attempt to attain that life.

This is the crucial difference. Religion offers a system that promises to lead to salvation one day. Jesus offers salvation as a gift, *now*. Everything after that becomes a joyful opportunity to express what is already ours, a celebration of salvation, not the method of it.

Occasionally someone who misses the point will say to me, "But Bruxy, how can you claim that religion is not the way to God when you are a pastor of a church? Aren't you a representative of religion?" The question arises out of the tendency to confuse form and substance. Once someone understands the substance of Christ's message, that no one religious form is the way to God, then we are free to express our love for Christ in a variety of forms. Forms themselves need not be shunned, but dependence on any one form for salvation does. The idolatry of forms has led to more division and suffering than anything else on the planet. But forms themselves are not the problem.

The problem with organized religion is not that it is organized. The problem with organized religion is that it is religious—believing that its own set of rules, regulations, rituals and routines are the exclusive way to God.

If I am right, then *the antidote to organized religion is not disorganized religion, but organized irreligion*—a collective effort to use organization and structure to help people encounter and experience the subversive spirituality of Jesus. Cups can be useful to hold water, as long as we remember that it is the water that refreshes and not the cup. Licking the cup leaves us unsatisfied.

This is the spirituality that I am inviting you to experience. It may mean the end of religion, but it is not the end of faith, expressing itself through love.

Q & EH?

1. In chapter 18 (Back to the Garden), I said, "For too long people have assumed that *religion* is how we connect with God, whereas *relationship* is how we connect with people. The original lesson of the Bible is that our connection with God should be a lot more like our relationships with other persons." How would your life change if you were more relational and less religious with God?

2. The value of forgiveness plays such a prominent role in the teachings of Jesus (see Matthew 5:23-24; 6:12,14-15; 9:2-8; 18:21-22; Mark 11:25; Luke 6:36-38; 15:11-32; 17:3-4). This makes sense within the context of Jesus' belief that our connection with God should be more like a mutual loving relationship between persons. Forgiveness is what makes ongoing relationship possible between imperfect beings (even if one *is* perfect!).

   • Do you sense your need of God's forgiveness in your relationship with him? Are there ways you have dishonored him and his creation?

   • Is there someone from whom you are withholding forgiveness? How might this affect your relationship with God?

3. Where does "church" fit in to the picture of someone who wants to follow the subversive spirituality of Jesus, but doesn't want to get trapped by religious tradition and prideful exclusivity?

   • What might be the advantages to being a committed member of a healthy, Jesus-following community (the meaning of "church")? List as many as you can think of.
   • What might also be the pitfalls of being a part of this same community?
   • What are some things we can do to guard against the pitfalls and maximize the advantages?

4. What, if anything, has this book addressed that could be helpful for your spiritual journey? What practical steps could you take to live differently in light of this?

———◆◆◆◆◆———

"Now go and learn the meaning of this Scripture: 'I want you to show mercy, not offer sacrifices.' For I have come to call not those who think they are righteous, but those who know they are sinners."

— MATTHEW 9:13, NLT

———◆◆◆◆◆———

The "Religion" God Likes

What religion do I preach? The religion of love.
— JOHN WESLEY

There is one passage in the New Testament that on first read seems to have something positive to say about "religion." The focus of the passage is the kind of lifestyle that should characterize people who follow Jesus. James the brother of Jesus writes an entire letter to the early Christian community to remind them of what their "religion" should be like. So what are the ceremonial trappings and the communal rituals supposed to be for the "religion" of Jesus?

> If you claim to be religious but don't control your tongue, you are fooling yourself, and your religion is worthless. Pure and genuine religion in the sight of God the Father means caring for orphans and widows in their distress and refusing to let the world corrupt you. (James 1:26-27, NLT)

What you have just read is the only clearly positive use of the word *religion* in the Bible. James does not place the emphasis on ritual and tradition, and not even on doctrinal or theological purity, but rather on practical, other-centered behavior. In summary, he says we should be:

- **constructive** rather than destructive in our words,
- **compassionate** in practical ways toward people in distress,

- **countercultural** in our daily life, refusing to simply follow the accepted norms of the majority (the "world") when those norms do not lead to a loving lifestyle.

The only "religion" that God accepts is *faith* (a trusting relationship with the person of God) expressing itself in practical loving action, as James goes on to explain fervently in his writing. For people who want to follow Jesus, the priority of rituals is replaced with other-centered relationship. And that's it. That's all. That's good religion in a nutshell, which in the end has little to do with what many people mean when they use the word *religion* today.

Now notice what James does *not* say in his letter to Christ-followers. He does not say that the only religion God appreciates is saying certain prayers a specified number of times each day, participating in the proper rituals, meditating in the right position, believing the right doctrines, attending the specified services, reading the appropriate books, memorizing the right texts, celebrating the right holidays, and so on. What people usually think of when they approach the topic of religion—the rules, rituals, and routines—are completely absent. Instead, the brother of Jesus concludes that God wants us to experience an intimate relationship with himself and then express that through a holistic lifestyle of compassion for others.

In one of his letters to a first-generation community of Christ-followers, the apostle Paul wrestled with the same issue of following the way of relationship or religion. His conclusion: "The only thing that counts is faith expressing itself through love" (Galatians 5:6). Faith, an intimate, trusting relationship with God, converted into love, that guiding force of other-centered care, compassion, and service. This is all that matters.

But where do we begin? Where do we turn to quench our thirsty souls?

Some religious or spiritual teachers counsel that we should learn to turn inward rather than reach out for a distant God outside ourselves. Their point is usually that people are already divine and that we simply need to become aware of our infinite nature.

As a Christ-follower I also turn inward, but for a different reason. Because I trust Jesus, I believe he has offered to indwell me by his Spirit, to interact with me, to guide me, and to continually reveal his love to me, from the inside out.

Jesus once told a spiritually thirsty woman he met by a well, "Anyone who drinks this water will soon become thirsty again. But those who drink the water I give will never be thirsty again. It becomes a fresh, bubbling spring within them, giving them eternal life" (John 4:13-14, NLT; also see 7:37-39). Notice, our first movement is to reach *out* to receive from Jesus, and by this our thirst is quenched. But it doesn't stop there. The water, the living Spirit that we drink, becomes a fountain inside us and we can then look *inside* to find this life-giving power.

I believe the Spirit of Christ comes to each of us and makes himself known in one way or another (John 12:32; 16:8), but he waits for us to reach out by faith. He may approach you through the Bible, through another person, through nature, through a book—maybe even this book, and maybe even in this moment. He has come to you. The next step is yours.

The information within the pages of this book is just that—information. Obviously, it won't change your life, raise your IQ, or make you a more attractive person. It will, quite frankly, do nothing for you but point the way. If the way of Jesus interests you, then you will have to take the next steps outside of these pages.

With that in mind, I would like to offer three suggestions of what your next steps might be:

First, *read this book again—slowly.* You now have the overview, so try digging deeper. Information at earlier stages in this book will mean more to you now that you have read to the end. Also, get a copy of the Bible in contemporary language and look up the Scripture references as you go. Read the context, appreciate the scandal. Try meditating on statements that stand out to you and/or journaling your thoughts and discoveries. Return to the question: What is the lesson in this *for me*? Try praying in response to the spiritual truths you discover. Talk to God about your life in relation to the things you are learning and how you might live differently in light of Jesus' teachings.

Second, *read through the Gospels*. Explore for yourself what Matthew, Mark, Luke, and John record about the life of Jesus and look for the big picture. If you like what you find, keep reading straight on through the New Testament. Keep a record of the insights you discover and the questions that arise.

Third, *seek out intentional community*. Find others who are asking the same questions and are willing to walk with you on this journey. Start a book club, create a spiritual discussion group, dip your toes in the water of a church community and ask lots of questions (like the ones you've been keeping a record of while reading through the Gospels). Since the spirituality of Jesus is relentlessly relational, it makes sense to process his teaching within relational contexts. Learn together, and when possible, take action together. Jesus does not call us to a privatized spirituality, but to an experience of spiritual family. John Stott writes, "God's purpose is not just to save isolated individuals, and so perpetuate our loneliness, but rather to build a new society, a new family, even a new human race, that lives a new life and a new lifestyle."[1]

In the early days of the Jesus movement, Christ-followers called each other "brother" and "sister" (see Romans 16:1; Philemon 2; James 2:15). This was not a way of being poetic and polite, but a reflection of what they really believed to be true. Many Christ-followers were disowned by their earthly families and friends, and eventually society in general turned on them, hunting down these peace-loving people and watching them die for sport. With the God of Jesus as their shared Father, they were truly family to each other. In all their struggles, they prayed not "My father who is in heaven," but "*Our* Father . . ." (Matthew 6:9).

Remember, ultimate truth is not found within a book—not this book, not any book. Jesus defined truth as a *person*—himself (John 14:6). To "know" truth is more than an intellectual exercise. It is a relational experience. My prayer for you is simply that "you will know the truth, and the truth will set you free" (John 8:32, NLT).

Origins of the Word *Religion*

Christianity is not a religion. Christianity is the proclamation of the end of religion, not of a new religion, or even of the best of all religions. . . . If the cross is the sign of anything, it's the sign that God has gone out of the religion business and solved all of the world's problems without requiring a single human being to do a single religious thing. What the cross is actually a sign of is the fact that religion can't do a thing about the world's problems—that it never did work and it never will.

— ROBERT FARRAR CAPON

There are always some people who feel like you've really made your case once you delve back into the ancient languages that the Bible was first written in. Without that, they feel like the story is incomplete. So for those of you who like that stuff, I offer this appendix.

The writers of the documents that we now call the New Testament wrote in first-century Greek—the most common written language for the known world at that time. They obviously wanted their message to be received by as many people as possible. There are two Greek words they used that we sometimes translate "religion" or "religious" in our English Bibles. Each one is used in a derogatory or a highly qualified sense.

Deisidaimonia means literally "dread of demons" and is used to refer to pagan religion. It might be better translated *superstition* or *superstitious* and is certainly not intended to be a complimentary word.

Threskeia primarily refers to the ceremonial worship of a deity and can be used to identify any externalization of someone's internal beliefs, whether positive or negative. Threskeia, then, refers to the outward trappings that may or may not be associated with any genuine faith. It is this word that James plays with in James 1:26-27, reframing it in terms of the love ethic of Jesus.

Jesus never calls people to threskeia religion (and certainly not deisidaimonia religion), but always emphasizes *faith* itself. The Greek word for "faith" is *pistis* in noun form and *pisteuo* in verb form, which is usually translated "believe" and sometimes "trust," because we do not have a natural verb form of the word "faith" in English.

How about our English word "religion"—where does that come from? The etymology of "religion" seems to have two Latin possibilities: *relegere*, meaning to read something over and over again; or *religare*, which is a combination of *re* (to return or to repeat) and *ligare* (to tie or to bind). Following this second option, religion can mean a returning to restraint; a fastening of the self to something that is considered important; a kind of anchoring or reconnecting. Positively understood, then, religion is "a reconnecting to something important." Negatively understood, religion simply means "a return to bondage." Obviously, I am referring to this negative usage in this book.

I understand that some people use the word "religion" to refer to a healthy outward expression of their inner faith, and that is wonderful. For the most part, when I look around me today, including looking over my shoulder at thousands of years of religious history, what I most often see in the name of religion is a ritualized return to bondage. The concept of religion has been closely associated with the repetitious tying of oneself to inherited beliefs and behaviors, traditions and theologies. Too often this leaves people mindlessly committed to the institution or clan that stewards the traditions, rather than the God who surrounds each of us with his love. Religion ties us down. Jesus came to set us free.

Language Today

*Those who lack discrimination may quote the letter of the
Scripture, but they are really denying its inner truth.*
— THE BHAGAVAD GITA

A book is written in words, but the words are not the important thing.
What matters is the message, the meaning conveyed through the words.
When people don't understand the message (or don't *want* to understand the message), they often fixate on the words themselves. In this
appendix, I want to challenge us all to avoid this divisive tendency.

Certainly, many people use the word "religion" today to refer to a
genuine, deeply rooted faith. Some people might talk about having a
"religious experience" as a way of referring to a spiritually transforming encounter with God. Now when someone tells me they are religious, I listen for the meaning and spirit behind their words rather
than argue about the words themselves. You would miss the intention
of this book if you used *The End of Religion* to fuel harsh judgment
toward anyone who called himself or herself "religious." All of us must
listen to the meaning behind the words people use, and I hope you are
doing the same with this book. *Every conversation demands a certain
amount of translation*, because of the simple fact that people use words
differently.

So watch out. It is possible to get into discussions, debates, and
arguments that are not really about anything of *substance* but are more
about the *labels* we use to describe our opinions. These arguments about

234 THE END OF RELIGION

words divide people needlessly and distract us all from our primary quest for truth.

The apostle Paul wrote words of advice to his coworker Timothy about this very issue. He counseled Timothy that one of his jobs as a spiritual leader should be to help people "stop fighting over words. Such arguments are useless, and they can ruin those who hear them" (2 Timothy 2:14, NLT; also see 1 Timothy 6:4; 2 Timothy 2:23; Titus 3:9).

Stop fighting over words. Pay attention to the *meaning*, to the *substance* of what people say, and then agree or disagree with that. I hope that you apply this principle while reading this book, or when engaging in spiritual discussions with others.

Words are human attempts to wrap labels around reality, and we must admit the imprecise nature of the enterprise from the outset, especially when talking about ultimate reality. This means we should approach spiritual discussions with large amounts of grace for others who might be struggling in their use of words to communicate their point of view.

"God is spirit," says Jesus (John 4:24), which means, among other things, that he is beyond form. Words are form. They compose information (*in-form*-ation). Our task is to use words as servants of our pursuit of truth without allowing words to become the master.

Perhaps this is one reason why Jesus commonly taught through storytelling rather than theological discourse (and why the Bible as a whole is a grand metanarrative of human spiritual discovery). In the words of Madeleine L'Engle, "Jesus was not a theologian; he was God who told stories."[1] Through parables, Jesus used narrative to show us truths about God and ourselves in a way that refuses to support our religious temptation to fixate on specific theological words.

Religious people like to hear certain words used in particular ways to make them feel secure and at home. Often, religious people emotionally bond with words as though they were the reality they label.

A man who heard me speak only once approached me afterward

to say that I didn't talk about God's sovereignty enough. In the one sermon he heard, I had spoken about God's kingdom, God's authority, and his loving guidance (what the word *sovereignty* refers to), but this man needed to hear the specific word *sovereignty* to feel good about the message.

Some people emotionally bond with words like *sin* (which means to miss the mark or fail to hit the intended goal) or *repentance* (which simply means to change your mind about something) or *holiness* (which means being set apart for a special purpose). Hearing these words used in books or sermons gives these people the emotional cues they need to feel good about what is being communicated. Synonyms will never do, nor would more literal translations of the original Bible word.

For the record, I don't make a practice of avoiding words like *sovereignty, sin, repentance,* or *holiness.* But neither do I feel the need to inject them into sermons or conversations in order to prove my biblical orthodoxy. Between you and me, I think these word-fixated people need to *repent* of their *sin* and live a *holy* life that is honoring to our *sovereign* God. (There, feel better?)

After a while, religious people can allow the words themselves to become part of the nonnegotiables of their faith, and when this happens, arguments ensue, usually about words rather than about reality. Take a course on the history of the Christian religion and you will see this principle in action over and over again, a legacy of division, persecution, and violence. At the very least, a religious obsession with theological phraseology can turn a thriving spiritual life into one that is dysfunctional and detached, deadened by an overdose of mental abstraction.[2]

Growing up in church circles, I have heard many Christians argue intensely for a specific interpretation of Scripture because Jesus uses *this* word and not *that* word to make his point in a particular Bible passage. Unfortunately, only a small minority of Christians thinks through the implications of the fact that Jesus likely spoke Aramaic, but his followers wrote down his teaching in Greek. We don't have the *words* of Jesus; we have the *Word* of Jesus.[3] In other words, we have Christ's message, preserved in his teaching and example, but we don't have the specific words he used to communicate that message.

Why did the New Testament authors write in Greek at the cost of recording the exact words of Jesus? The reason seems pragmatic. Quite simply, Greek was the most widely read language of their day. For the writers of the four biblical Gospels, it was more important to get the message out there than to have the exact words of Jesus known by all. Obviously, it was the *message* they wanted us to focus on, not the specific words.[4]

Unfortunately, religious people often bond with certain words as though they hold magical power to produce spiritual results. The consequence is a strange form of linguistic idolatry that is expressed in a religion of pseudoacademic debates rather than brotherly and sisterly love. By writing the Gospels in Greek, the first followers of Jesus help us understand that it is the message that matters, and not the magical use of specific religious words.

Through stories and word pictures, Jesus calls all listeners to consider the meaning of his message. In reflecting on its meaning, he invites us to discover the God who loves us beyond anything words could ever express.

Grasping the Gospel

*If only there were evil people somewhere insidiously committing
evil deeds and it were necessary only to separate them from the
rest of us and destroy them. But the line dividing good and
evil cuts through the heart of every human being. And
who is willing to destroy a piece of his own heart?*

— ALEKSANDR SOLZHENITSYN

This world is indescribably beautiful. This world is ugly to the core.
This world is full of life, love, and joy. This world is unspeakably sad.
The printing press is an amazing invention of human creativity. The
newspapers we print detail our human depravity. I take a walk outside
and can't help but think of nature as a work of divine art, until I see a
lion slowly pulling down a gazelle on a television nature show. Ours
is a world where the words *child* and *pornography* are used in the same
sentence. What is wrong with this world?

To some extent, all religion is an attempt to answer that question:
what is wrong with this world? Religion grows out of our intuitive
sense that we need to correct something that is incomplete or out of
sync about our human experience. Every religion labels this problem
differently, from attachment to ignorance to bad karma, but what
unites all religions is the offer to help humanity overcome whatever
the problem is.

The Bible labels our problem *sin*, and this is good news, because
sin can be straightforwardly dealt with through something called

forgiveness. Sin is a relational block, requiring a relational remedy. It takes the form of any attitude or action that orients us away from rather than toward God. We sin whenever we "miss the mark" of following God's loving will for our lives.[1] Sin is egocentricity: self-centered rather than God-centered living. When we choose this path, we cause pain — to others, to God, to ourselves, and to all of creation. N. T. Wright comments: "'Sin' is a power let loose in the world, a deceptive and corrosive parasite that has entwined the whole human race in its tentacles and is slowly choking it to death."[2]

Because we are all connected in creation (Adam was made out of the ground and Eve was made out of Adam, and, ever since, all people have been "made" out of other people), when we sin we affect all creation on some level. In a sense, sin is like spiritual pollution, slowly raising the level of nature's dysfunction. The Bible records that when Adam and Eve first sinned, creation itself started to malfunction (see Genesis 3:17-18), and now "the whole creation groans and suffers" (Romans 8:22, NASB).

There are strains of modern spirituality that live in denial about any negative aspect of our human nature. People who subscribe to these ways of believing want only to think of our humanity in terms of light and love and perfection. But I think any spirituality that is afraid to look at the dark side of humanity, to really stare it in the face, is in deep denial and fundamentally insecure.

Yes, to be human is to be a glorious image-bearer of the divine. But we are not only image-bearers of God, we are broken image-bearers, and we need help to put ourselves and this world back together again. Both aspects of our humanity must be held together if we want to think clearly about who we are and what we need. Even though Jesus attributed infinite worth to the people he met (see Matthew 10:29-31), he was never in denial about their sin. In fact, Jesus believed that the origin of evil, the locus of all our problems, is the human heart (Mark 7:20-23). Looking back over the last century, I am inclined to agree.

Each of us carries around inside him or her the seeds of war, murder, rape, and theft. We can choose to nurture our hate, our lust, and our envy and help create a world full of victimization and poverty, or we can repent of—that is, turn away from—that side of our soul and ask God to help us grow in Christlikeness. Jesus helps us regain the image of God in us.

The first step in getting help is admitting something is wrong. Interestingly, Jesus never went out of his way to convince people they were sinners. He kept his eyes open for those people who were brave enough to admit their internal struggles and then offered them the help they needed. This is why his followers were rarely religious people, but admitted "sinners." When the religious leaders pointed this out as though it were a design flaw in his movement, Jesus responded: "Healthy people don't need a doctor, but sick people do. I didn't come to invite good people to be my followers. I came to invite sinners" (Mark 2:17, CEV).

Of course, Jesus knew that all people are, on some level, "sick." But he also knew that only some people are secure enough or honest enough or shattered enough to admit it. When we are ready to admit our sickness, we are ready for the cure.

In the Old Testament times, animal sacrifices were used to physically and graphically portray the damage sin does spiritually. These sacrifices were more symbolic than effectual, foreshadowing a coming reality.

> The law is only a shadow of the good things that are coming —not the realities themselves. For this reason it can never, by the same sacrifices repeated endlessly year after year, make perfect those who draw near to worship. Otherwise, would they not have stopped being offered? For the worshipers would have been cleansed once for all, and would no longer have felt guilty for their sins. But those sacrifices are an annual reminder of sins. It is impossible for the blood of bulls and goats to take away sins. (Hebrews 10:1-4)

Jesus became the reality, the substance, of which the sacrificial system was merely a shadow (see also Colossians 2:16-17). The temple sacrifices were like graphic dramas, all finding their fulfillment in Jesus. Fascinatingly, all ancient religions were, in their own way, pointing toward the same reality, because, as Karen Armstrong records: "Animal sacrifice was a universal religious practice in the ancient world."[3]

The early Christ-followers believed that Jesus had become a kind of cosmic sin sponge, absorbing the sin of this world into a single point and, in so doing, offering to reverse the process of decay for those who would trust in him and eventually for all of creation. Sin is rooted in habitual self-preservation rather than self-giving. Jesus undoes the power of sin through his grand act of self-sacrifice, of life-giving-away love: "God made him who had no sin to be sin for us, so that in him we might become the righteousness of God" (2 Corinthians 5:21). Through Jesus, God absorbs our sin and, if we are willing to accept it, we can absorb his perfection. And so, God himself becomes the solution to the world's problem, inviting us all into reconciled relationship with him: "God was in Christ reconciling the world to Himself, not counting their trespasses against them, and He has committed to us the word of reconciliation" (2 Corinthians 5:19, NASB).

This message is called "the gospel," which means "good news." It is exactly that—good news. God has done the work of saving us from our own sin and selfishness. He simply asks that we trust him on this—that we have faith in him: "God loved the people of this world so much that he gave his only Son, so that everyone who has faith in him will have eternal life and never really die. God did not send his Son into the world to condemn its people. He sent him to save them!" (John 3:16-17, CEV).

So we could summarize the gospel as the good news message that God became one of us to:

- show us his love (see Luke 15:11-32; John1:1-3,14-18; 3:16; 5:19; 14:7-10; Romans 5:8; 2 Corinthians 5:19; Philipians 2:5-7; Colossians 1:19-20; 2:9; 1 John 3:16; 4:9-11);

- save us from sin (see Matthew 9:1-8; John 1:29; 12:46-47;
  Acts 13:38-39; Romans 3:21-26; 1 Corinthians 15:1-4;
  2 Corinthians 5:21; Ephesians 2:5; 1 Timothy 1:15; 1 Peter
  2:24);
- shut down religion (see Matthew 5:17; John 3:17; 14:6-10;
  Acts 17:24-28; Romans 6:23; 8:1-4; 10:4; Galatians 2:16; 5:1;
  Ephesians 2:8-10,14-15; Colossians 2:13-17; 1 Timothy 2:5;
  Hebrews 8:13).

Some people are not ready for this message. They may stumble over any one of these aspects of the gospel:

- **Love**: They think of themselves as unlovable and have trouble accepting that the Creator of the universe is gaga about them.
- **Sin**: They don't want to think of themselves as needing forgiveness for sin.
- **Faith**: They think salvation by simply trusting God is too easy, too simple. They don't want to let go of their more intricate religious systems.

I remember "stumbling" over the simplicity of this one Bible passage, in which the apostle Paul tries to explain to a group of Christians how they came to be God's children: "For by grace you have been saved through faith, and this is not your own doing; it is the gift of God — not the result of works, so that no one may boast" (Ephesians 2:8-9, NRSV).

That is amazing grace. Because of his love, his grace, God has reached out to us. Grace is an internal reality for God. The fact that his motivation for saving us is internal means that there is nothing we could do to make him love us any more than he does now, and nothing we could do to make him love us any less.

I remember looking at my daughters when they were babies sleeping in their cribs. There was nothing they were doing nor could do to make me love them any more or any less. The love I had for them and still have for them was and is involuntary. It simply is. This is the heart of God toward us.

Notes

PREFACE: A REST FROM RELIGION

1. From *How to Talk Dirty and Influence People* by Lenny Bruce, quoted in Darren John Main, *Spiritual Journeys Along the Yellow Brick Road*, 39.
2. Stott, *Why I Am a Christian*, 35.
3. McLaren, *The Secret Message of Jesus*, xi.

INTRODUCTION: THE HOLY HAND GRENADE

1. Heschel, *I Asked for Wonder*, 40.
2. In the book of Revelation, chapters 21 and 22, the final state of humankind is described as a return to the world as God intended. The author highlights the fact that there is no "temple" in this brave new world (see Revelation 21:22). The temple was the institution that connected people with God in first-century Israel, the focus of the rituals of sacrifice and cleansing. But in this final state, says Revelation, God himself will act as the temple. No more forms, no more structures, no more rituals to connect us with God. The story of the Bible, then, is the story of the many detours and sidetracks taken by humanity on its way back to intimate union with God, and the many ways God helped us along the way. Ultimately, it is the story of God not just revealing a solution but becoming the solution; not just pointing to a pathway, but becoming the pathway back to the garden. This is the meaning of Jesus.
3. The apostle Paul picks up on this imagery in his writings, suggesting that Christ-followers today should be actively involved in carrying on the same mission (see 2 Corinthians 10:3-5).
4. I have researched and taught on the Jesus-never-existed theory. Although fascinating at points, I find that too many of its proponents tend toward putting agenda ahead of facts. I agree with historian Paul L. Maier, professor of ancient history at Western Michigan University, who writes in the introduction to his book *In The Fullness of Time* (Grand Rapids: Kregel, 1998), "Of all religious beliefs in the world, past or present, none

have more thoroughly based themselves on history than Judaism and Christianity. The divine-human encounter in the biblical faiths always involves claims about real people, living in real places, who acted in real events of the past, many of which are also cited in secular ancient history" (xv). The bottom line for me is if the historical Jesus wasn't the origin of the radical actions, stories, and teachings of the New Testament, then I want to find out who invented it all—and follow that person! For now, I'm happy to call that person "Jesus."

5. For more on the canonical Gospels as Greco-Roman biographies, see Richard Burridge's *What Are the Gospels?*.

6. Perhaps you have heard theories about how the institutional church selected for the Bible only those gospel writings that seemed to support the church's authority while rejecting other gospels that seemed more subversive, more threatening to the church's position of power (the gospels of Thomas, Mary, Peter, Judas, etc.). About this I would like to point out two facts that often get lost in the shuffle of these more sensational theories: First, we should remember that the Gnostic gospels are dated to at least the second and third centuries (much later than the canonical Gospels). So the biblical Gospels are just the better choice for getting back to the Jesus of history. Secondly, the Jesus of the biblical gospels of Matthew, Mark, Luke, and John is no supporter of any religious system of power, as we will discuss in part 2 of this book. If the institutional church was trying to do away with any sense of the radical, subversive, and irreligious teachings of Jesus, it did a pretty lousy job. So I am committed to pouring my energies into mining the biblical Gospels for all they have, rather than diffuse my energies into late-dating Gnostic texts.

7. I'm sorry for the violent imagery here, but it has a purpose. I'm not talking about blowing up people, buildings, or structures, but the human dependence on those people, buildings, and structures as codependent systems of salvation. It's a metaphor. Work with me. One friend told me that for her the pin-pulling started when she meditated on John 1—a chapter of the Bible which includes thoughts that, if allowed to rise like yeast in your quiet mind, will potentially "blow your mind" in the best possible way.

8. Although God clearly plays the role of both Father and Mother to his people in the Bible, he is never called "Mother" directly. The biblical deity is a Father God with a Mother's heart. (For feminine imagery of

God in the Bible, see Deuteronomy 32:18; Psalm 90:2; Isaiah 42:14;
45:9-10; 49:15; 66:12-13; Matthew 23:37; John 3:5-6; James 1:18; 1 Peter
2:2-3.)

9. Vanier, *Becoming Human*.

PART ONE

CHAPTER ONE: WATER, WINE, AND SCANDAL

1. Sayers, *Creed or Chaos?*, 6–7.
2. There are some Christians who claim that Jesus would never create
   anything alcoholic and that the "wine" Jesus makes in this story must
   actually be unfermented grape juice. The theory is fascinating, but biblically unsupportable. The same Greek word for wine in this passage (*oinos*)
   is used elsewhere in the Bible to refer to a liquid that has the ability to
   purify a wound (see Luke 10:34) or cause drunkenness (see Ephesians
   5:18) or even addiction (see Titus 2:3). These are qualities of alcohol, not
   vitamin C. In the Septuagint (the Greek translation of the Hebrew Bible
   that was read and quoted by the New Testament authors), *oinos* most
   often translates *yayin*, which is the Hebrew word for fermented wine (as
   opposed to *tirosh* or *mishreh*, usually meaning unfermented juice or juice
   that is not yet fully fermented). Also see Luke 7:33-34 where, unlike John
   the Baptist, Jesus garners the reputation among the religious conservatives of his day of being a "drunkard" because he drinks *oinos*. The Bible
   (Old Testament and New Testament) often warns against the potential
   negative effects of alcohol and teaches against drunkenness, but does not
   mandate complete abstinence. That is a choice left for every individual.
3. In first-century, Roman-occupied Israel, Jews were waiting for this
   prophet like Moses who would be their deliverer (see John 1:21). Jesus
   offered deliverance, but from a deeper slavery than political oppression
   — slavery to our own sin and selfishness, and slavery to religion.
4. The writers of the New Testament used a Greek word for the kind of love
   Jesus shows us: agape. It means a love that is inclusive, embracing, and
   unconditional.
5. Yes, my search took me beyond the precepts and traditions of the
   Christian religion, but not beyond the Bible. Instead, I realized that the
   Bible itself contains the best challenge to religion we could hope for. As I
   explain in the introduction, no book is more threatening to religion, and

no version of Jesus being studied in today's world is more subversive than the biblical Jesus.

CHAPTER TWO: RELIGION, SPIRITUALITY, AND FAITH

1. See "Spirited Away: Why the End Is Nigh for Religion," the cover story of British newspaper *The Times*, November 4, 2004, at http://www .timesonline.co.uk/tol/life_and_style/article502475.ece. Also take a look at this online article by Paul Chamberlain, "The Quest for Spirituality," Faith, September/October 1997, http://www.christianity.ca/faith/faith- and-thought/2003/11.001.html; and books like *The Spiritual Revolution: Why Religion Is Giving Way to Spirituality*, by Paul Heelas and Linda Woodhead. Certainly, some people might talk about having a "religious experience" as a way of referring to a deeply spiritual encounter with God. People use words like *spiritual* and *religious* differently. Now, when someone tells me they are religious, I listen for the meaning and spirit behind their words rather than argue about the words themselves, which is why in this chapter I define how I use these words. *Every conversation demands a certain amount of translation*, because of the simple fact that people use words differently. Watch out. It is possible to get into discussions, debates, and arguments that are not really about anything of *substance* but are more about the *labels* we use to describe our opinions. These arguments about words divide people needlessly, and distract us all from our primary quest for truth (see 2 Timothy 2:14,23; 1 Timothy 6:4).

2. To be sure, there is a good kind of religion that God approves of, but, unfortunately, it is much less popular than the kind I describe in this chapter. We will discuss this good kind of religion in the epilogue.

3. God always prefers the creative approach to problem solving. And notice that in the Bible God rarely uses the same approach twice. Religion, on the other hand, thrives in repetition.

4. The language of a second birth was a metaphor used by first-century Judaism to explain what happened to a Gentile who converted to the faith of Moses. For a Gentile to become a Jew meant entering into a brand-new life, totally discontinuous with his or her past. It meant entrance into a new life and a new family. So it is all the more shocking that Jesus should tell a religious Jew that he must be "born again."

5. Heschel, *I Asked for Wonder*, 22.

CHAPTER FOUR: CHAMBER OF HORRORS

1. For more on the positive contribution of Christians throughout the past two millennia, see Vincent Carroll and David Shiflett, *Christianity on Trial: Arguments Against Anti-Religious Bigotry*; Alvin J. Schmidt, *How Christianity Changed the World*; and Philip Jenkins, *The New Anti-Catholicism: The Last Acceptable Prejudice*.

2. The apostle Paul seems to be making the same point about the hypocrisy of his own religious background in Romans 2:17-24.

3. Willard, *The Great Omission*, x.

4. Wall, Sampley, and Wright, *The New Interpreter's Bible*, 10:427.

5. Ellerbe, *The Dark Side of Christian History*, 65. Although this record is obviously embellished (other versions of this tale record blood up to the knees of the horses, not the riders), the fact that Christians played up rather than played down the horrific violence of this event tells us even more about Christian attitudes at the time.

6. Moynahan, *The Faith*, 239.

7. That the promise of personal gain in this life was necessary to motivate the Cathar Crusade illustrates an important point. In many cases of religious violence, politics and personal gain are the root cause while religion simply offers the justification. The formula is simple: Politics + Religion = Increased Violence.

8. Innocent III, quoted in "The Holy Inquisition," http://www.geocities.com/christprise/holy-inquisitions.html.

9. Within the horror of this and every story of church-sponsored terror, real Christ-followers emerge, such as the thousands of Christians who willingly gave their lives rather than turn over the hunted Cathars.

10. Moynahan, 283.

11. During my seminary days I learned to appreciate the amazing mind of Reformed theologian John Calvin. His intellectual brilliance led to an entire system of theological thought named after him (Calvinism). But Calvin's doctrinal emphasis left him with a moral blind spot, as his encouragement of the execution of suspected heretic Michael Servetus demonstrates. The fact that Calvin advocated "mercifully" beheading Servetus rather than burning him alive (as was done) is little comfort. History demonstrates that "orthodox" theology alone rarely leads to the spiritual fruit of "love, joy, peace, patience, kindness, goodness, faithfulness, gentleness, and self-control" (Galatians 5:22-23). To all who follow in Calvin's intellectual footsteps, the apostle Paul says, "If we live by the

Spirit, let us also be guided by the Spirit. Let us not become conceited, competing against one another, envying one another" (Galatians 5:25-26, NRSV).

12. "The Burning Times" is a semiaccurate reference, since, unlike other "Christian" countries, in England and New England suspected witches were usually hanged. See Brian Moynahan, *The Faith: A History of Christianity*, 498.

13. To be clear, I am not arguing against the doing of theology (theology is the application of philosophical thought to the topic of God). Jesus invites his followers to love God with their entire mind (see Matthew 22:37; Mark 12:30). But theology alone is not the basis for Christian unity.

14. Fowler, *Christianity Is Not Religion*, 100.

15. McLaren, *The Secret Message of Jesus*, 85.

16. Clouser, *Knowing with the Heart*, 32.

17. Also consider this description of Christ's return from a contemporary best-selling Christian novel. Remember that these words bring comfort and encouragement to countless believers: "Men and women, soldiers and horses, seemed to explode where they stood. It was as if the very words of the Lord had superheated their blood, causing it to burst through their veins and skin. . . . Their innards and entrails gushed to the desert floor, and as those around them turned to run, they too were slain, their blood pooling and rising in the unforgiving brightness of the glory of Christ" (Tim LaHaye and Jerry Jenkins, *Glorious Appearing*, 225–226).

CHAPTER FIVE:
TAKING THE "MENTAL" OUT OF FUNDAMENTALISM

1. Harris, *The End of Faith*, 33.

2. Ali, "Jihad Explained." Note: (S) denotes Sall-Allahu 'alayhi wa sallam, meaning "peace and blessings of Allah be upon him."

3. For an insider critique of Islam, see Irshad Manji, *The Trouble with Islam Today*.

4. Dugger, "Religious Riots Loom over Indian Politics."

5. Jesus, in keeping with his Jewish roots, affirms the infinite value of this life now, not as a punishment for our past failure but as an expression of divine love. We are not here because we are working off our bad karma from past lives we cannot even remember. Our existence in this

dimension at this time in this form is an expression of divine love, not divine punishment.

6. Juergensmeyer, *Terror in the Mind of God*, 114.

7. Jainism is a clear and extreme exception, instructing complete nonviolence even toward animals and some plant life where eating the edible part of the plant (for example, root vegetables) would destroy the entire plant.

8. Paul Hill was friends with the Reverend Michael Bray, who expressed similar beliefs in his book *A Time to Kill*. While serving time on death row, Hill wrote his own book titled *Mix My Blood with the Blood of the Unborn*, detailing his thought processes that led him to gun down the two men. See www.armyofgod.com for more details. It is a deeply disturbing Web site.

9. McLaren, *The Secret Message of Jesus*, 212.

PART TWO

CHAPTER SIX: TAKING ON THE ESTABLISHMENT

1. The historian N. T. Wright highlights three of these as crucial for understanding the impact of Jesus on his first-century world — the law, the land, and the temple.

2. N. T. Wright argues that the verb *entrusted* in Romans 3:2 grows out of Paul's understanding that Israel was not given God's teachings as an end destination, but was entrusted with a message they were supposed to deliver to all people.

3. Placher, *Jesus the Savior*, 93

4. William C. Placher and Beverly Roberts Gaventa, foreword to *We Are the Pharisees* by Kathleen Kern, 10.

CHAPTER EIGHT: A FENCE AROUND THE LAW

1. Notice that Jesus highly values the Jewish Scriptures as "the commandment of God" and "what God said" even though, as we saw in the last chapter, he often broke those very commandments. Jesus never taught that Scripture was the problem, but that the problem is religious people's legalistic way of interpreting and applying it.

2. The Pharisees treated their oral Torah as seriously as the written Torah, believing that God gave Moses the oral Torah at the same time as the

written Law to help explain, expand, and enhance it (see The Mishnah, Abot 1:1). Jesus opposed this view as dangerously exalting the traditions of people to the level of the teachings of God. The Pharisees believed "A more strict rule applies to the teachings of scribes than to the teachings of Torah" (The Mishnah, Sanhedrin 11:3, Jacob Neusner translation). In other words, the commentary, interpretations, and applications given by the teachers of the Law should be given precedence over Scripture itself. This interpretation leaves the door wide open for human traditions and points of view to be made authoritative in the lives of religious people. In an attempt to remove any mystery from the Bible, religious leaders craft official explanations for every obscure passage and those explanations, doctrines, and traditions then become sacrosanct. Eventually, those who claim loudest to follow the Bible can end up following their own way instead of God's way.

3. Other examples of tradition eclipsing Scripture would include prohibitions against drinking and dancing which are common in some Christian circles. Religious bans on drinking and dancing serve as fences around the biblical teaching against drunkenness and seduction.

4. For a terrific book that compares Jesus' criticism of the Pharisees with present-day Christianity, see Tom Hovestol, *Extreme Righteousness*, 1997.

CHAPTER NINE: FAMILY VALUES

1. For example, see Sirach 12:1-7.

2. Regarding Jewish hatred of Samaritans, see Luke 9:52-56.

3. Jesus says they were not Pharisees, but a "priest" and a "Levite" (or "Temple assistant"), both of whom served as part of the temple sacrificial system.

4. And even if they were going the other way and coming home from serving in the temple, as temple staff, to be in contact with a corpse would still be a direct violation of the strict rule of Torah — not to mention make them unsuitable for contact with their families for one week.

5. Robert Farrar Capon points out that the battered and bleeding man, stripped of all marks of racial and religious identity, is a foreshadow of Jesus himself, soon to be battered beyond recognition as a Jew, let alone as the Messiah, the liberator of Israel (*Kingdom, Grace, Judgment*, 216). When Jesus dies hanging on a Roman cross, he dies as a man for all humanity, not just as a Jew for Israel.

6. The listeners might also have expected the story to end with a Pharisee passing by and becoming the hero, since their tradition of the elders taught that saving a life took precedence over all other rules of Torah. See Brad H. Young, *Jesus the Jewish Theologian*, 166–167.

7. Kraybill, *The Upside-Down Kingdom* (1990), 184.

8. Josephus, 262.

9 Culpepper, *The New Interpreter's Bible*, 9:229–230. Also see Sylvia C. Keesmaat, "Strange Neighbors and Risky Care," in *The Challenge of Jesus' Parables*, 280–281, for a further discussion of the offensive symbols used in this story. The hits just keep on coming.

10. This seventeen-mile stretch of lonely road was called "the path of blood" in the days of Jesus.

11. Samaritans also followed Torah, and so the same risk of defilement from touching a dead body was present for this Samaritan as well, with ritual uncleanness extending also to his animals and merchandise. So here we see one man who is willing to step outside of his own religious box, beyond the borders and boundaries, in order to love his enemy.

12. Culpepper, 232.

13. Also see Luke 12:51-53.

CHAPTER TEN: THY KINGDOM COME

1. King, "The Casualties of the War in Vietnam."

2. Certainly refusal to fight is not the only distinguishing mark of Christ-followers. Jesus elsewhere teaches that his followers would be known by their love (see John 13:35). But it is hard to love your brother or your enemy as Christ commands when you are trying to kill him in battle.

3. There are some teachings of Jesus that are hard to understand. His peace teaching is not in that category. It is hard to live out, sure, but it is not hard to understand. Read it for yourself in Matthew 5:38-47 and Luke 6:27-36. Sadly, in an attempt to soften the radical nature of Jesus' peace teaching, some Christian leaders have scoured the New Testament to find something that might hint at Jesus being more open to violence as a valid methodology for his disciples to use. For instance, I've heard more than a few Christian preachers try to justify religious violence by referring to Jesus' words: "Do not think that I came to bring peace on the earth; I did not come to bring peace, but a sword" (Matthew 10:34, NASB). In context, however, Jesus is warning his followers that if they follow him and apply his teachings others may be violent toward them. But he does

not advise his own followers to become violent. To the contrary, he goes on to call all who want to follow him to take up their own cross, not their own sword—in other words, we should be willing to die for our faith, but not kill for it. Another passage that those Christians who are grasping at straws to validate violence sometimes refer to is a cryptic passage where Jesus advises his followers to take up swords (see Luke 22:35-38), but in light of everything else Jesus has said on the topic, a thoughtful exegesis must lead us to ask if he is speaking symbolically. As it turns out, this is clearly the case. When the disciples misunderstand Jesus and reach for literal swords, he shuts down the conversation—"That is enough" (22:38) or "Enough of that" (msg). Then, when Peter tries to use one of the swords to defend Jesus when he is arrested, Jesus rebukes Peter for his misunderstanding—"Put your sword back where it belongs. All who use swords are destroyed by swords" (Matthew 26:52, msg). Of course, the obvious observation is that people who don't take up a sword can still die by the sword. True. But Jesus is not opposed to his followers dying for their cause. He is opposed to them killing for it.

4. The Greek word translated "within" in this verse could also be translated "among." Either way, Jesus is pointing out that God's kingdom transcends the territory of one particular nation, building, or system.

CHAPTER ELEVEN: SACRED SPACE

1. N. T. Wright, lecture given in Toronto, summer of 2006.
2. Capon, *Kingdom, Grace, Judgment*, 1.
3. Placher, *Jesus the Savior*, 94.
4. See 2 Samuel 12:13; 1 Kings 8:46-50; Jonah 3:10; Psalm 40:6.
5. See 1 Samuel 15:22; Micah 6:6-8.
6. Wills, *What Jesus Meant*, 76.
7. This doesn't mean that there is something wrong with having favorite places that are personally meaningful to enhance our sense of God's presence in our lives. Jesus had his favorite places where he would withdraw to pray (see Luke 5:16) and expected his followers would have the same (see Matthew 6:6). The problem comes when we grow dependent on any one place to meet with God and forget that his presence surrounds and indwells us at all times.

CHAPTER TWELVE: SUBVERSIVE SYMBOLS

1. This is a process I hope to write about in my follow-up book, *The Irreligious Life*.

CHAPTER THIRTEEN: THE DAY RELIGION DIED

1. My focus in this book is on the life and death of Jesus. I intend to make the resurrection and its implications for Christ-followers the focus of a future work.

2. This is unlike any other great spiritual leaders, most of whom died of natural causes. Consider Moses, Buddha, Confucius, and Muhammad. In each case, their life and teachings are important, which were simply brought to a close by their death, something that, in and of itself, is insignificant. But in the case of Jesus, his life and teachings point toward his death as being central to his mission. And so, his life ends in violent slaughter in his early thirties, having so enraged the authorities with his scandalous teaching.

3. Wills, *What Jesus Meant*, 59.

4. The writers of the Bible viewed the resurrection of Jesus as God's affirmation that the crucifixion really did accomplish its work. As in Matthew 9:1-8, where Jesus heals a man physically as proof that he has healed him spiritually by forgiving all of his sin, so God works an observable miracle of resurrection to affirm that the spiritual miracle of forgiveness of sin, apart from the religious system, has taken place for all.

5. Of course, no one believed that God's presence was restricted to the temple (see 2 Chronicles 2:6), but that God somehow manifested his presence, his glory, within the Holy of Holies in greater measure, as he used to do when talking with Moses (see Exodus 25:21-22; 30:6; 33:9; Leviticus 16:2).

6. On the topic of Jesus taking away our sins through his death, see Isaiah 53:5-12; John 1:29; 1 Corinthians 15:3; 2 Corinthians 5:21; Galatians 1:4; 1 Peter 2:24.

7. Borg, *The Heart of Christianity*, 94–95.

8. Stott, *Why I Am a Christian*, 62–63. Also see his wonderful work *The Cross of Christ*, 335.

PART THREE

CHAPTER FOURTEEN: WHO DO YOU THINK YOU ARE—*GOD*?

1. Stott, *Why I Am a Christian*, 35.
2. Stott, *Why I Am a Christian*, 36.
3. This is very different from, say, Gautama Buddha. The story is told that when dying he was asked by some of his friends how they should perpetuate his memory. He answered that they should not focus on remembering him, but that his teaching was all that mattered. True or not, this is certainly in keeping with the thrust of Buddhist teaching. In most religions, you can remove the founder and still have the religion. You can remove Buddha from Buddhism and still have the Four Noble Truths and the Eightfold Path. You can remove Muhammad from Islam and still have the Five Pillars of Action and the Six Articles of Belief.
4. Lewis, *Mere Christianity*, 52.
5. Kinlaw, *Let's Start with Jesus*, 69.
6. This directional thrust of God coming to us is not a one-time historical event, but an ongoing reality. His Spirit, "the Spirit of Christ" (Romans 8:9; 1 Peter 1:11), continues to come to us, offering conviction of his love and our need (see John 16:8,13-14).

CHAPTER FIFTEEN: GOD OR SON OF GOD?

1. See discussion in chapter 9.
2. On God living and working through Jesus' crucifixion see Romans 5:8; 2 Corinthians 5:19; Colossians 1:19-20. In Romans 3:21 the apostle Paul calls Jesus the *hilasterion*, a Greek word sometimes translated "mercy seat" or "atonement cover" (see Hebrews 9:5), referring to the place on the lid of the ark of the covenant between the cherubim where the divine presence would descend and speak with Moses (see Numbers 7:89). Once a year on the Day of Atonement (Yom Kippur), the high priest would sprinkle the blood of a sacrifice on the hilasterion to atone for the sins of Israel (see Leviticus 16:14-16). The hilasterion, then, represents the point of contact between the divine and human, a place where sacrifice is offered and forgiveness is granted. If Jesus is the hilasterion, then God is meeting us through him, becoming the sacrifice for us, offering mercy, and making the old sacrifice-forgiveness system obsolete. The cross of Christ really is now the "mercy seat."
3. I wrote this illustration before our family got Toby the Wonder Dog from

the pound. Snowball still gets lots of attention, but we no longer feel the need to walk him on a leash.

4. The embodiment of God in human flesh has implications for Christ-followers today. The New Testament teaching that Christ-followers make up the "body of Christ" (1 Corinthians 12:27) is not just a poetic image. It is a call to manifest the Spirit of Christ, God's Spirit of sacrificial love, to our world in tangible, demonstrable, observable, embodied ways. When we make self-sacrificing choices by investing our energies in serving the poor, helping the needy, and befriending the lonely, we become the physical presence of Christ to others in life-giving ways. Then we are truly living like the sons and daughters of God: the physical manifestation of Jesus on earth today—the body of Christ.

CHAPTER SIXTEEN: WORD OF GOD

1. See Jeremiah 17:9 and Mark 7:20-23.
2. Notice the ongoing present tense of Romans 5:8.
3. Borg, *The Heart of Christianity*, 80.
4. Thomas Adams, http://www.zaadz.com/quotes/Thomas_Adams.
5. I believe God "commissioned" the book to be written—it is not of merely human origin, but a human-divine partnership, which is always God's "MO" (see 2 Timothy 3:16-17). But the enduring, eternal, preexisting Word of God comes from his heart to us in Jesus, not the Bible (see John 1:1,14,18).
6. Barclay, *The Mind of St. Paul*, 87.
7. Also see Matthew 5:17, where Jesus claims to be the fulfillment of the Bible's purpose.

CHAPTER SEVENTEEN: LOVE INSTEAD OF LAW

1. The apostle Paul makes the same assumption in Ephesians 5:29. I understand that some people with specific mental dysfunctions do not love themselves well, but this is not the point of Jesus' use of the concept of self-love.
2. Rideout, *The Truth You Know You Know*, 6.
3. Likewise, when I park my car at a meter, I try to put in just enough money to cover my time parked in that space. It never occurs to me to put extra money in the meter in order to pay for other people who come after I'm gone, even though I am always happy when I arrive at a meter that still has time left on it. When my mind is in law mode rather than

love mode, it's all about me.

CHAPTER EIGHTEEN: BACK TO THE GARDEN

1. Yes, the Bible records God giving Adam and Eve one rule: "You must not eat from the tree of the knowledge of good and evil" (Genesis 2:17). Why have even one rule? And why put that tree in the garden in the first place? I think the answer lies in the nature of love. Real love necessitates choice. If love is not chosen, it is not love. For instance, if I were the last man on earth, the fact that my wife tells me "You're the man for me, Bruxy" would hardly encourage my heart. The beautiful thing about love is that, given other options, the lover still chooses the beloved. God chose Adam and Eve. He could have created anyone, but he chose them, just as he chose us (see Ephesians 1:4). For them to fully reflect the image of God and to really love God as he loved them, they had to be given the choice to take a different path. Of course any choice that moves us away from God rather than toward him will eventually lead to some form of death, for God is the source of all life. But God did not force Adam and Eve to choose life, or else it would not be a real choice. For more on this one rule of the Garden of Eden and why Adam and Eve broke the rule and the enduring results of that choice, see Gregory Boyd's book *Repenting of Religion*.

2. Ironically, the specific item of Torah under question in Matthew 19 is an allowance in Deuteronomy 24 that lowered the standard of morality. The way of love that Jesus proclaims always raises the ethical standard. Now—and this is key—notice the implication of Jesus' teaching in this situation. If Jesus blames the low standard of Old Testament law on human hard-heartedness, and he simultaneously calls his followers to a higher standard, the implication is that Jesus is offering a remedy for our heart condition. He called that remedy the Holy Spirit.

CHAPTER NINETEEN: IT'S TIME TO GROW UP

1. See other biblical injunctions to grow up in Hebrews 5:12-6:1 and 1 Peter 2:2-3.

CHAPTER TWENTY: RELIGION VERSUS RELATIONSHIP

1. The same Greek word for faith is also translated "believe" or "belief" in our English Bibles.

2. Willard, *The Divine Conspiracy*, 318.

3. Borg, *Jesus*, 20–21.

4. Boyd, *Repenting*, 195–208

5. In Matthew 12:30 and Luke 11:23, Jesus appears to teach the exact opposite, saying "Whoever is not with me is against me." But as is often the case, the context is key. In these examples Jesus is involved in a confrontation with the religious leaders and his rebuke is directed at them (see Matthew 12:24). But in Mark 9:41 Jesus is talking about people who are trying to sincerely follow Jesus, even if they don't belong to the "right" group.

CHAPTER TWENTY-ONE: SO WHAT?

1. Although *skubalon*, used in Philippians 3:8, means "dung," it can also be used to refer to garbage or something that is useless by comparison, which is why some translations render the word as "refuse" or "garbage" or "rubbish."

2. I respond the same way when asked about our specific denomination, Brethren in Christ, even though I am a huge fan of this wonderful segment of the body of Christ.

3. This does not mean that we do not plan for the future, but we hold our future plans with a gentle grip, knowing that the outcome is not in our hands. See Matthew 6:25-34 and James 4:13-16.

EPILOGUE: THE "RELIGION" GOD LIKES

1. Stott, *Why I Am a Christian*, 111.

APPENDIX B: LANGUAGE TODAY

1. L'Engle, *Walking on Water*, 54.

2. To be clear, I am not suggesting that theology is unimportant. This book is an exercise in a kind of theological discourse. Jesus says we should love God with our minds as well as our hearts (see Mark 12:30). What I am saying is that Christians must never treat theological study as our stairway to heaven. Finding the right words and phrases to express faith in Christ is not what saves us. For instance, as a Christian, I believe in the doctrine of justification by faith. But I do not believe that I am saved by believing in the doctrine of justification by faith. I am saved by Jesus (see 1 Timothy 2:5). In words attributed to Karl Barth, "Jesus does not give recipes that show the way to God as other teachers of religion do. He is himself the way."

3. This disparity between the original words spoken and the written words of the Bible applies to the four gospels that record the life and teachings of Jesus. In other New Testament books, such as the letters of Paul, we do have the authors' original words since they wrote in Greek what they meant to say in Greek.

4. There is an added benefit of the Bible not recording the specific words of Jesus that becomes evident when we contrast the Bible with the Qur'an. Muslims believe that the Qur'an records the specific words of Allah in their original Arabic. This means that fluency in Arabic is necessary for a person to get the most out of the Qur'an, for these are believed to be the very words of God. Those who do not read Arabic are always at a disadvantage, for no translation into another language is considered to be a "real" Qur'an. In fact, one of the evidences that Muslims use as "proof" that the Qur'an is inspired by God is how beautifully it reads—in Arabic—a proof that is not available to non-Arabic speakers. But thankfully, the Bible invites us to appreciate the beauty of its message, not its Aramaic, Hebrew, or Greek. Rather than be an academic message fit for scholars fluent in ancient languages or a secretive message for Gnostic mystics who alone know the keys to unlock the mystery, Jesus taught that his message is accessible to all, even children.

APPENDIX C: GRASPING THE GOSPEL

1. The Greek word most commonly used for "sin" in the New Testament is *harmartia*, which means to "miss the mark."

2. Wall, Sampley, and Wright, *The New Interpreter's Bible*, 10:554.

3. Armstrong, *The Great Transformation*, xv.

Bibliography

Ali, M. Amir, PhD. "Jihad Explained." Institute of Islamic Information and Education. No. 18. 2006. http://www.iiie.net/Articles/tabid/54/TID/18/cid/1/Default.aspx.

Armstrong, Karen. *A Short History of Myth.* New York: Canongate Books, 2005.

_____. *The Great Transformation: The Beginning of Our Religious Traditions.* New York: Alfred Knopf, 2006.

Baker, Mark D. *Religious No More: Building Communities of Grace and Freedom.* Downers Grove, IL: InterVarsity Press, 1999.

Barclay, William. *The Mind of St. Paul.* London: Fontana Books, 1965.

Barnett, Paul W. *Jesus and the Logic of History.* Edited by D. A. Carson. Vol. 3 of *New Studies in Biblical Theology.* Downers Grove, IL: InterVarsity Press, 1997.

Barth, Karl. *The Humanity of God.* Richmond, VA: John Knox Press, 1960.

Bock, Darrell L. *Studying the Historical Jesus: A Guide to Sources and Methods.* Grand Rapids, MI: Baker Academic, 2002.

Borg, Marcus J. *The Heart of Christianity: Rediscovering a Life of Faith.* San Francisco: HarperSanFrancisco, 2003.

_____. *Jesus: Uncovering the Life, Teachings, and Relevance of a Religious Revolutionary.* San Francisco: HarperSanFrancisco, 2004.

Borg, Marcus J., and N. T. Wright. *The Meaning of Jesus: Two Visions.* San Francisco: HarperSanFrancisco, 1999.

Boyd, Gregory A. *Repenting of Religion: Turning from Judgment to the Love of God.* Grand Rapids, MI: Baker Books, 2004.

Boyd, Gregory A., and Edward K. Boyd. *Letters from a Skeptic: A Son Wrestles with his Father's Questions About Christianity.* Colorado Springs: Cook Communications, 1994.

Buckman, Robert. *Can We Be Good Without God?: Behavior, Belonging and the Need to Believe.* New York: Viking, 2000.

Burridge, Richard A. *What Are the Gospels?: A Comparison with Graeco-Roman Biography*. Grand Rapids, MI: Eerdmans Publishing Company, 2004.

Capon, Robert Farrar. *Between Noon and Three: A Parable of Romance, Law, and the Outrage of Grace*. San Francisco: Harper and Row, 1982.

_____. *Kingdom, Grace, Judgment: Paradox, Outrage, and Vindication in the Parables of Jesus*. Grand Rapids, MI: Eerdmans Publishing Company, 2002.

Carroll, James. *Constantine's Sword: The Church and the Jews*. New York: Mariner Books, 2001.

Carroll, Vincent, and David Shiflett. *Christianity on Trial: Arguments Against Anti-Religious Bigotry*. San Francisco: Encounter Books, 2002.

Cawthorne, Nigel. *Witches: History of a Persecution*. London: Arcturus Publishing, 2004.

Chalke, Steve, and Alan Mann. *The Lost Message of Jesus*. Grand Rapids, MI: Zondervan, 2003.

Clouser, Roy. *Knowing with the Heart: Religious Experience and Belief in God*. Downers Grove, IL: InterVarsity Press, 1999.

Collinson, Patrick. *The Reformation: A History*. New York: Modern Library, 2004.

Culpepper, R. Alan. *The New Interpreter's Bible*. Vol. 9. Nashville: Abingdon, 1995.

Dennett, Daniel C. *Breaking the Spell: Religion as Natural Phenomenon*. New York: Viking, 2006.

Dubay, Thomas, SM. *The Evidential Power of Beauty: Science and Theology Meet*. San Francisco: Ignatius Press, 1999.

Dugger, Celia W. "Religious Riots Loom over Indian Politics." *New York Times*. July 22, 2002. http://www.genocidewatch.org/Indianriots27July2002.htm.

Ellerbe, Helen. *The Dark Side of Christian History*. Orlando, FL: Morningstar and Lark, 1995.

Fowler, James A. *Christianity Is Not Religion*. James A. Fowler, 1998. http://www.christinyou.net/pages/notrel.html.

Green, Joel B., and Mark D. Baker. *Recovering the Scandal of the Cross: Atonement in New Testament and Contemporary Contexts*. Downers Grove, IL: InterVarsity Press, 2000.

Green, Michael. *Who Is This Jesus?*. Nashville: Thomas Nelson, 1990.

Groothuis, Douglas. *Wadsworth Philosophers Series: On Jesus*. Toronto: Thompson Wadsworth, 2003.

Habermas, Gary R. *The Historical Jesus: Ancient Evidence for the Life of Christ*. Joplin, MO: College Press Publishing Company, 2001.

Harris, Sam. *The End of Faith: Religion, Terror, and the Future of Reason*. New York: W. W. Norton and Company Inc., 2004.

Heelas, Paul, and Linda Woodhead. *The Spiritual Revolution: Why Religion Is Giving Way to Spirituality*. Oxford: Oxford University Press, 2005.

Heschel, Abraham Joshua. *I Asked for Wonder: A Spiritual Anthology*. Edited by Samuel H Dresner. New York: Crossroad Publishing Company, 2003.

Hovestol, Tom. *Extreme Righteousness: Seeing Ourselves in the Pharisees*. Chicago: Moody Press, 1997.

Jenkins, Philip. *The New Anti-Catholicism: The Last Acceptable Prejudice*. New York: Oxford University Press, 2003.

Josephus, Flavius. *Josephus: The Essential Writings*. Edited by Paul L. Maier. Grand Rapids, MI: Kregel Publications, 1988.

Juergensmeyer, Mark. *Terror in the Mind of God: The Global Rise of Religious Violence*. Berkeley and Los Angeles: University of California Press, 2003.

Kaiser, Walter C., Jr. *The Christian and the "Old" Testament*. Pasadena, CA: William Carey Library, 1998.

Keesmaat, Sylvia C. "Strange Neighbors and Risky Care." In *The Challenge of Jesus' Parables*. Edited by Richard Longenecker. Grand Rapids, MI: Eerdmans Publishing Company, 2000.

Kern, Kathleen. *We Are the Pharisees*. Scottdale, PA: Herald Press, 1995.

Kimball, Charles. *When Religion Becomes Evil*. New York: HarperCollins, 2002.

King, Martin Luther, Jr. "The Casualties of the War in Vietnam." Speech, Los Angeles, CA, February 25, 1967.

Kinlaw, Dennis F. *Let's Start with Jesus: A New Way of Doing Theology*. Grand Rapids, MI: Zondervan, 2005.

Kraybill, Donald B. *The Upside-Down Kingdom*. Waterloo, ON: Herald Press, 2003.

_____. *The Upside-Down Kingdom*. Scottdale, PA: Herald Press, 1990.

LaHaye, Tim, and Jerry Jenkins. *Glorious Appearing*. Wheaton, IL: Tyndale, 2004.

L'Engle, Madeleine. *Walking on Water: Reflections on Faith and Art*. Wheaton,

IL: Harold Shaw Publishers, 1980.

Lewis, C. S. *Mere Christianity*. San Francisco: HarperSanFrancisco, 2001.

Maier, Paul L. *In the Fullness of Time: A Historical Look at Christmas, Easter, and the Early Church*. Grand Rapids, MI: Kregel, 1998.

Main, Darren John. *Spiritual Journeys Along the Yellow Brick Road*. Tallahassee, FL: Findhorn Press, 2000.

Manji, Irshad. *The Trouble with Islam Today: A Muslim's Call for Reform in Her Faith*. Toronto: Vintage Canada, 2005.

McCracken, David. *The Scandal of the Gospels: Jesus, Story, and Offense*. New York: Oxford University Press, 1994.

McLaren, Brian D. *The Secret Message of Jesus: Uncovering the Truth That Could Change Everything*. Nashville: W Publishing Group, 2006.

Miles, Jack. *Christ: A Crisis in the Life of God*. New York: Alfred A. Knopf, 2001.

Moynahan, Brian. *The Faith: A History of Christianity*. New York: Image Books, 2002.

Nelson-Pallmeyer, Jack. *Jesus Against Christianity: Reclaiming the Missing Jesus*. Harrisburg, PA: Trinity Press International, 2001.

_____. *Is Religion Killing Us?: Violence in the Bible and the Quran*. New York: Trinity Press International, 2003.

Neusner, Jacob. *Judaism When Christianity Began: A Survey of Belief and Practice*. Louisville, KY: Westminster John Knox Press, 2002.

Nolan, Albert. *Jesus Before Christianity*. Maryknoll, NY: Orbis Books, 2000.

Placher, William C. *Jesus the Savior: The Meaning of Jesus Christ for Christian Faith*. Louisville, KY: Westminster John Knox Press, 2001.

Rideout, N. Kenneth. *The Truth You Know You Know: Jesus Verified in Our Global Culture*. Nashville: NDX Press, 2005.

Sayers, Dorothy L. *Creed or Chaos?: Why Christians Must Choose Either Dogma or Disaster*. Manchester, UK: Sophia Institute Press, 1974.

Sanders, E. P. *The Historical Figure of Jesus*. New York: Penguin, 1993.

Schmidt, Alvin J. *How Christianity Changed the World*. Grand Rapids, MI: Zondervan, 2004.

Siefrid, Mark A. *Christ, Our Righteousness: Paul's Theology of Justification*. Edited by D. A. Carson. Vol. 9 in *New Studies in Biblical Theology*. Downers Grove, IL: InterVarsity Press, 2000.

Stott, John. *Why I Am a Christian*. Downers Grove, IL: InterVarsity Press, 2003.

_____. *The Cross of Christ*. Downers Grove, IL: InterVarsity Press, 1986.

_____. *Focus on Christ.* New York: Collins, 1979.

Tice, Rico, and Barry Cooper. *Christianity Explored.* Waynesboro, GA: Authentic Media, 2002.

Twiss, Miranda. *The Most Evil Men and Women in History.* London: Michael O'Mara Books, 2002.

Vanier, Jean. *Becoming Human.* Compact disc of lectures by Jean Vanier at Massey College, Toronto, 1998. Toronto: CBC Audio, 2001.

Van Voorst, Robert E. *Jesus Outside the New Testament: An Introduction to the Ancient Evidence.* Grand Rapids, MI: Eerdmans Publishing Company, 2000.

Wall, Robert W., J. Paul Sampley, and N. T. Wright. *The New Interpreter's Bible.* Vol. 10. Nashville: Abingdon, 2002.

Weis, René. *The Yellow Cross: The Story of the Last Cathars' Rebellion Against the Inquisition.* New York: Vintage Books, 2000.

Willard, Dallas. *The Divine Conspiracy: Rediscovering Our Hidden Life in God.* San Francisco: HarperSanFrancisco, 1998.

_____. *The Great Omission: Reclaiming Jesus' Essential Teachings on Discipleship.* New York: HarperCollins Publishers, 2006.

Wills, Garry. *What Jesus Meant.* New York: Penguin, 2006.

Wright, N. T. *Jesus and the Victory of God.* Minneapolis: Fortress Press, 1996.

_____. *The Challenge of Jesus.* Downers Grove, IL: InterVarsity Press, 1999.

_____. *Simply Christian: Why Christianity Makes Sense.* New York: Harper Collins, 2006.

Witherington, Ben, III. *The Christology of Jesus.* Minneapolis: Fortress Press, 1990.

Yancey, Philip. *The Jesus I Never Knew.* Grand Rapids, MI: Zondervan, 1995.

Yoder, John Howard. *The Politics of Jesus.* Grand Rapids, MI: Eerdmans Publishing Company, 1999.

Young, Brad H. *Jesus the Jewish Theologian.* Peabody, MA: Hendrickson Publishers, 1995.

About the Author

BRUXY CAVEY is the teaching pastor of The Meeting House—a church for people who aren't into church. This multisite community in the Greater Toronto area shares the same teaching and vision: to create safe places for spiritual seekers to ask questions and develop thoughtful faith. Bruxy's accessible style, historical rigor, and refreshing candor make him a popular guest on television and radio programs and at universities across Canada. He lives in Hamilton, Ontario, with his wife, Nina, and three daughters, Chelsea, Chanelle, and Maya; their dog, Toby; and their hamster, Snowball.

For more information, visit www.TheEndOfReligion.org.

CHECK OUT THESE OTHER GREAT TITLES FROM NAVPRESS!

Dangerous Faith

Joel Vestal
ISBN-13: 978-1-60006-197-4
ISBN-10: 1-60006-197-4

Today's world is filled with stories of oppression, war, famine, and extreme poverty. A Christian's mandate is clear: Feed the hungry, free the oppressed, and offer light in dark places. Can each believer truly make a difference? The stories and insights of *Dangerous Faith* will challenge indifference and encourage you to actively express compassion.

Daughters of Eve

Virginia Stem Owens
ISBN-13: 978-1-60006-200-1
ISBN-10: 1-60006-200-8

Virginia Stem Owens invites you to examine some of the fascinating stories of biblical women. Many of the issues they faced (violence, multiple marriages, manipulation, motherhood) are issues of urgent importance to women today. Much has changed since the first woman walked the earth, but at least one thing remains the same: Being a woman is as challenging as it ever was.

The Year I Got Everything I Wanted

Cameron Conant
ISBN-13: 978-1-60006-145-5
ISBN-10: 1-60006-145-1

Cameron Conant was on the verge of a new life full of promise. After a painful divorce, he set out to pursue a new job opportunity and a promising relationship. But just one year later, Cameron was unemployed and reeling from two failed relationships. *The Year I Got Everything I Wanted* provides a fresh parallel to the book of Ecclesiastes, as Cameron searches for meaning and purpose.

Visit your local bookstore, call NavPress at 1-800-366-7788, or log on to www.navpress.com to purchase.